Embracing
CHRISTIAN
SPIRITUALITY
WITH
EMOTIONAL
CORE
THERAPY

Robert A. Moylan, LCPC

ISBN: 0692711775

ISBN 13: 9780692711774

Library of Congress Control Number: 2016907939

Robert A. Moylan, Lisle, IL

CONTENTS

DISCLAIMER

This book details the author's personal experiences with and opinions about mental health and relationships. The author and publisher are providing this book and its contents on an "as is" basis and make no representations or warranties of any kind with respect to this book or its contents. The author and publisher disclaim all such representations and warranties of merchantability and healthcare for a particular purpose. In addition, the author and publisher do not represent or warrant that the information accessible via this book is accurate, complete, or current.

The statements made in this book are not intended to diagnose, treat, cure, or prevent any specific condition or illness. Please consult with your own physician or mental healthcare provider regarding the suggestions and recommendations made in this book.

Neither the author nor the publisher will be liable for any damages arising out of, or in connection with the use of this book. This is a comprehensive limitation of liability that applies to damages of any kind, including (without limitation): compensatory, direct, indirect, or consequential damages; loss of data, income or profit, loss of or damage to property and claims of third parties.

You understand that this book is not intended as a substitute for consultation with a licensed healthcare practitioner, such as your physician or therapist. Before you begin any healthcare program or change your lifestyle in any way, you will consult with your physician or healthcare provider to ensure that you are in good health and that the examples used in this book will not harm you.

This book provides content related to mental health and relationships. As such, your use of this book implies your acceptance of this disclaimer.

Embracing

CHRISTIAN
SPIRITUALITY
WITH
EMOTIONAL
CORE
THERAPY

A Simple and Effective Method
to Empower the Mind

BY ROBERT A. MOYLAN, LCPC

ACKNOWLEDGEMENTS

I would like to thank my daughter, Anna, who brings me great joy. I also want to thank all my clients who have worked hard in their therapy sessions. A special thanks to my editor, Mike Valentino. His patience and expertise were invaluable during the writing of this book.

AUTHOR'S NOTE

The goal of this book is to reach anyone who desires to learn how to live a full life of vitality and energy. To live life to its fullest, without any regrets. One of the best ways to do this is to get the most out of each day you live. One of the best ways to get the most out of each day you live is to not have the debilitating feelings of fear, anger, and grief inhibit or cripple your lifestyle. For Christians, this includes prayer and a connectivity with God through Jesus. Emotional Core Therapy can help people with that important facet of their life. It is the simplest and most effective behavioral psychology treatment available worldwide for most relationship stress including addictions, depression, anxiety, anger, personality disorders, childhood emotional trauma, sports psychology, and marital therapy. ECT is not a religiously based approach, and will work even if you do not adhere to any faith tradition. However, for people whom the Christian faith is a crucial aspect of their lives (the Pew Research Center says 70% of Americans identify as Christians), ECT will be a perfectly natural fit. It never asks you to do or say anything that would be contrary to the gospel. In fact, it will help strengthen your beliefs as it lifts up your spirits and allows you to clear the clutter from your mind, therefore seeing both the physical and spiritual dimensions of your life as if through new eyes. Yes, it may even lead you to a spiritual renewal and awakening that you had never before thought possible.

How does one test the validity of a psychology or self-help book? What you have to do is list the top ten to twenty stressful events in your life. With the 8 step ECT Flowchart in my book you can process almost any relationship stress that occurs in life. It is really quite that simple. All you have to do is reflect on the ten to twenty most stressful events in your life. Then write those events down on a sheet of paper. Once you have read Emotional Core Therapy (the process sinks in through repetition best) you can then process your ten to twenty stressful events through the ECT Flowchart. You will then have verified evidence that ECT is the only behavioral psychology approach that is so simple you can use it for almost any relationship stress in your life. No other psychology approach, religious teaching, or educational process can claim these results.

Up till now, the vast majority of counselors, social workers, psychologists, psychiatrists, priests and ministers have been relying on psychology techniques/approaches such as Rational Emotive Therapy/ REBT, Cognitive Behavioral Therapy/CBT, Dialectical Behavioral Therapy/ DBT, Acceptance and Commitment Therapy, Psychoanalysis, Motivational Interviewing, 12 Steps, and even religious teachings to heal people. In this book, we will offer approaches to ECT that come from Christian perspectives. The focus will be Christianity in general, not any specific group or denomination. A major goal of Christianity is the quest for inner peace, tranquility, and happiness, which is one of the many reasons why it blends so smoothly with ECT, which at its core is designed to help each individual learn to quiet their mind.

ECT uses many of the same techniques as some of the other aforementioned psychological approaches listed above. However, ECT also includes my own unique research and findings and condensed the ECT process to eight steps. With ECT, there is renewed hope that addictions and mental health issues can be treated more effectively throughout the world.

How can one prove the effectiveness of a psychology approach to assess the capability for treating human relationship stress? Can we measure a psychology approach like we do with a major league pitcher throwing a fastball, or an Olympic runner racing in a 100-yard dash? Unfortunately, we cannot measure any psychology approach, including ECT, over an extended period of time. When I say extended period of time I mean three to six months or longer. Why? Too many variables exist that would adversely affect an accurate measurement. For example, training of mental health professionals varies. Educational and aptitude level of people vary greatly. Resources and environments vary from person to person. Each person varies in how they experience life stresses. Also, each person carries new stress that would adversely impact any study.

Again, the only effective way to truly measure any psychology approach is to list ten to twenty stressful events that a person faces in their daily lives. Then try and process them through whatever psychology approach, religious teaching, or educational approach that you currently use. Then do the same with my eight step ECT Flowchart. There will be your evidence. Only ECT effectively treats the root cause of human relationship stress. How does ECT do this? There exists a cause and effect relationship with stress. The ECT Flowchart depicts how the natural state of stress occurs. For every relationship stress a person encounters on a daily basis, one thing happens with certainty every time. What is that? One of the four true feelings, joy, grief, fear, or relief will arise and occur. These four temporary feelings cause stress to humans by altering one's central nervous system.

You can't deny, suppress, or ignore the four true and authentic feelings for very long without hurting yourself in some fashion. The four true feelings will happen no matter what you do on a daily basis. Illegal drugs and alcohol can only alter, dull, or dampen, your five senses and four feelings. That's why emotionally healthy people realize that, for the most part, taking drugs or medications won't change the conditions you face in life. Only your perception changes. Altering your mind and yourself with depressants and stimulants will only delay your emotional growth. Why? The four true feelings are with us hourly and daily our whole lives.

ECT is one of the most important discoveries in the history of the field of psychology and mental health. Why? With ECT we have discovered the root cause of relationship stress! The root cause of stress is the temporary arousal of the four true feelings. With the eight step ECT Flowchart, we now have a psychology approach that can effectively treat the root cause of relationship stress for humans. The good news is that ECT is the simplest and most effective psychology approach to treat nearly all psychological disorders and relationship stress that people face. The exceptions are some cases where permanent physical or psychological damage has occurred. Even activities such as throwing out your back lifting a heavy object or changing your tennis swing can be understood clearer using the ECT Flowchart.

I've never encountered a stressful human interaction that I wasn't able to comprehend how I feel using the eight step ECT Flowchart. In some rare occasions it is hard to distinguish the exact variable that caused you stress. For example, hitting a golf shot out of a deep rough on a downhill slope on a cold windy day. You mishit the shot badly. Often, the variables are too many to accurately know what caused you stress. What you can always recognize is the true and authentic feeling of grief or fear that follows taking the poor shot. This is similar to a college fraternity boy who has a hangover from drinking vodka, beer, smoking marijuana, and staying up late. He is not exactly sure what caused the pain, but he sure knows he feels the pain/ grief.

Every stressful event in a person's life (for example, divorce, financial loss, spousal abuse or neglect, parenting stress, supervisor yelling at you at work, gambling addiction) can all be traced back to the four feelings. Why not honor and learn from these four feelings? Why run away from them or disconnect from them? That is the focus of ECT! When you learn from emotions you become more aware of what limitations your body and mind has regarding the four emotions.

As a Christian, ECT will likely become a part of your prayer life, meditation and spiritual devotional time. We will see in this book practical examples of how followers of Christ can use ECT to enrich and fulfill their everyday lives.

Think of it this way. Two gold diggers are on a sandy beach hunting for precious metals. One miner has a metal detector that detects hundreds of metals, many of them useless. The other miner has a metal detector that can detect the four true minerals of value (for example, gold, silver, platinum, and aluminum). Who has the simpler and more effective method of mining? Obviously the second gold digger is more efficient. The same goes with emotions. We will show in the book there are hundreds of names for emotions. When you can reduce the number down to the four true emotions, a person will have a much easier job learning from them. Why? The four true and authentic emotions serve as a navigation tool or compass in life by helping you choose healthy relationships that bring you joy and leaving unhealthy relationships that bring you grief and fear. All my clients that leave therapy successfully have real power and confidence in their lives. Why? They leave therapy knowing they can have a relaxed, meditative state of being, very close to what is termed "mindfulness" in psychology circles. Then when any type of stress occurs in their lives they have the full confidence in the eight step ECT Flowchart. They know that they can identify, process, and release this situational stress and get back to a normal relaxed state of being. No other psychological, religious, or educational approach can do this as they are continually redirecting you away from your true emotional state. For my Christian clients, this hourly and daily emptying of emotions takes on even more meaning. Why? They have learned to have a truly spiritual and peaceful relationship with Jesus that is their predominant state of being. Then, whenever they feel bodily stress and discomfort, they can have full trust in the Eight Step ECT Flowchart to identify and treat any situational stress they encounter in life and regain their treasured spiritual relationship with Jesus. This has been one of the goals of all Christians since the time of Christ. Now this goal of spiritual unity with Jesus has become very attainable for nearly all Christians.

Another example I use is a school teacher in a school ground. One teacher has to supervise 150 children. Another teacher has to supervise four children. Who has the easier job? Obviously the school teacher who supervises four children has the less stressful job. We breakdown needs in our

ECT Flowchart down to four categories also. The needs and demands people face from their relationships are what cause stress. So when we simplify the needs and emotions for people we can help them learn more quickly and effectively.

Stress, in the form of the four true feelings comes hourly and daily for people. The key point for all healthy individuals is to learn to cathartically release these emotions. Perhaps you are thinking, aren't prayer and meditation supposed to do that? Prayer and meditation are indeed important for religious people, and ECT is not designed to replace these virtuous practices. Instead, ECT works right alongside these spiritual pursuits like a perfect match. ECT is the most inclusive psychology approach worldwide as it can incorporate any psychological technique that is proven to help release emotions. I give over 20 examples in my books on how to successfully release emotions. Mental Health professionals will learn to love ECT as many of the techniques they have learned in school (EMDR, biofeedback, hypnosis, art therapy, etc.) can be incorporated into ECT when problems occur with clients. Even common ways of relaxing such as yoga, Pilates, sitting in a warm Jacuzzi, listening to music on headphones, etc., can be easily incorporated into the eight step ECT Flowchart.

The key concept to understand here is portability or deliverability. What can the mental health professional easily teach and deliver to the patient that he can easily digest and learn and apply in his daily life. The goal of ECT is autonomy and independence for the client.

ECT is now being used throughout many parts of the world. Since joining Linkedin last year, I have now been endorsed by thousands of professionals across the globe. ECT was the top rated book in two categories (Emotions and Mental Health) on Amazon in 2014. Approximately ten thousand people have read and reviewed ECT without any major criticisms of the ECT process. Why? It works as a process to identify and release stress if used correctly. This has included people from many various faith traditions, along with those who practice no particular religion. In fact, part of the beauty of ECT is that it can work for anyone, regardless of your upbringing, beliefs or spiritual disposition. As you will discover in this book, ECT fits perfectly with Christianity. The support system of churches blends in seamlessly, too, as does prayer. All three work together to help improve the overall condition of your body, mind and soul.

Currently, I teach ECT to medical and mental health professionals both online and in person for continuing education units (CEUS) for their license renewal. This includes psychologists, social workers, counselors, nurses, marriage and family therapists, physical therapists, chiropractors, massage therapists, and several other professions. ECT is approved by a dozen United States licensing boards for continuing education credit and renewal.

I have a strong commitment to better the world and make it a more peaceful place. The psychology field can unite us as human beings if we work together and educate teens and adults on learning to really love themselves and love others.

My hope is to have all religious organizations and mental health providers utilize ECT and bring people throughout the world closer together as human beings.

Lastly, remember that knowledge is power! You and your loved ones all have been hurt and in pain from emotional stress of some kind from a relationship. It is only human nature to be a bit "stressed out" from time to time. With ECT you will now have the tools to help yourself and others. ECT is the closest thing I know to an "Emotional Fountain of Youth". When you learn to cleanse your soul daily you can keep yourself feeling youthful all your life.

This book teaches you a simple step approach that brings one closer to mastering the mind. The ECT Flowchart that you see on the adjacent page will be placed throughout the book at the end of each chapter. This will be beneficial for those visual learners who want to monitor their growth and progress in order to measure how much you have learned about the ECT process. A simple suggestion would be to use a highlighter or black marker at the end of each chapter to note which sections of the ECT flowchart you are able to comprehend. The author does not want to cause the reader undo stress so he emphasizes that oftentimes we do some of the ECT steps automatically or instinctively.

A great way to learn psychology techniques is through storytelling. This book will utilize that approach as it makes learning the process of Emotional Core Therapy even simpler and more enjoyable. For readers who learn through a more interactive style, there will be a list of important concepts at the end of each chapter.

EMOTIONAL CORE THERAPY AND THE SCIENTIFIC METHOD

As you begin the journey to understand the Emotional Core Therapy process please keep in mind the scientific method. The scientific method is a process for creating models of the natural world that can be verified experimentally. The scientific method requires making observations, recording data, and analyzing data in a form that can be duplicated by other scientists. The subject of a scientific experiment has to be observable and reproducible. Observations may be made with the unaided eye or any other apparatus suitable for detecting the desired phenomenon. The apparatus for making a scientific observation has to be made on well-known scientific principles. The Scientific method requires that theories be testable. If a theory cannot be tested, it cannot be a scientific theory. The scientific method requires and relies on direct evidence. This means evidence that can be directly observed and tested. Scientific experiments are designed to be repeated by other scientists and to demonstrate unequivocally the point they are trying to prove by controlling all the factors that could influence the results.

Source (Scientificpsychic.com/Scientific Method)

Here are the four steps to the scientific method and the Emotional Core Therapy process.

1) Observation made both visually and with scientific equipment

Stress occurs on the mind and body. There exists a cause and effect relationship with stress. Oftentimes this stress can be uncomfortable for humans.

2) Formulation of a hypothesis to explain the phenomenon in the form of a causal mechanism/method/approach.

Many psychology methods (REBT, CBT, ACT, DBT, etc.), religious approaches (this would include the 12 steps, etc.), and educational programs (Smart Recovery) have attempted to fully and completely explain via a model, how this cause and effect relationship with stress occurs. Up until this point in time, we have not had a model in the world that can successfully depict how this stress occurs each and every time. To their credit, many of these methods partially work and have contributed greatly to humanity. See Wiki.com for information on all the psychology methods and techniques mentioned in this book. With the invention/discovery of Emotional Core Therapy (ECT) we now have a psychology method that accurately can depict this causal relationship between stress and humans through Mr. Moylan's Eight Step Emotional Core Therapy Flowchart. Complete explanations of each of the eight steps of the ECT Flowchart exist in the accompanying book. With ECT, we now have a psychology approach that identifies and treats the root cause of psychic stress. The root cause of psychic stress is the temporary arousal of one of the four true emotions (joy, grief, fear, and relief). ECT also shares and borrows many psychological techniques from the aforementioned approaches.

3)   Test the hypothesis.

The Eight Step flowchart has been tested thousands of times by Mr. Moylan in many venues including his clinical practice as well as in his role of training other professionals. The ECT process works accurately to depict the situational stress affecting humans. Anytime someone experiences psychological stress, aspects of each of the eight steps of the Emotional Core Therapy Flowchart will be utilized and affected. Why does this phenomenon happen when one experiences stress? The Emotional Core Therapy process highlights and identifies the key components of the root cause of stress. Anyone can test the model which is utilized extensively in this book.

4)   Establish a theory based on repeated verification of the results.

Billions of people suffering relationship stress can be helped by Emotional Core Therapy. Every effort needs to be made to ensure people suffering from stress have access to this model and accompanying treatment program in this book. Every effort needs to be made to educate the human population on the ECT process as all humans suffer stress from time to time. Because of the inclusiveness of Emotional Core Therapy, many effective psychology techniques that have been demonstrated to release stress can be incorporated into ECT. It takes time and will to learn and apply ECT. Behavioral psychology, including ECT has some limitations, which are addressed in Mr. Moylan's work. Some of the requirements to effectively learn ECT are a level of cognition generally at or above a high school level. Also, those with long term physical or psychological damage may not be able to utilize all steps effectively.

One of the most powerful benefits of ECT is its ability to incorporate any psychology or religious method that can successfully release emotions. The following approaches are some of the many techniques that have been shown to successfully release emotions. Gestalt Therapy, role playing, psychodrama, art therapy, music therapy, hypnosis, EMDR, biofeedback, Reiki, pet therapy, journaling, Mindfulness, some aspects of prayer, yoga, verbalization of emotions, etc., as part of the eight step process. View Wiki.com for detailed explanations of these techniques. Humans release stress in many ways and it is important to work from a person's worldview and utilize techniques that may be familiar to them.

The ECT process works just like entering data into a computer. You enter your own situational stress into the Emotional Core Therapy Model to relieve stress and get back to a peaceful centered sense of well-being. Relationship stress generally varies from person to person which is step one of the ECT Model. Generally, each individual experiences the four true feelings differently which is step six of the ECT model. People release their stress in a variety of ways which is step seven of the ECT model. And finally, everyone meditates/relaxes in a variety of ways which is step eight step eight of the process. Because of the many varied ways human beings experience and release stress, the ECT model and accompanying book will offer readers a user friendly approach to treating stress in their lives. For Christians this means regaining that spiritual connection with Christ.

ECT Flow Chart

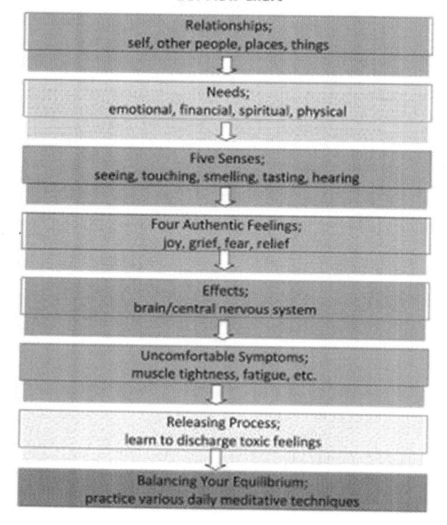

Relationships;
self, other people, places, things

⬇

Needs;
emotional, financial, spiritual, physical

⬇

Five Senses;
seeing, touching, smelling, tasting, hearing

⬇

Four Authentic Feelings;
joy, grief, fear, relief

⬇

Effects;
brain/central nervous system

⬇

Uncomfortable Symptoms;
muscle tightness, fatigue, etc.

⬇

Releasing Process;
learn to discharge toxic feelings

⬇

Balancing Your Equilibrium;
practice various daily meditative techniques

INTRODUCTION
Overview of ECT Process

If you're human, keep reading. This book is about you. Yes, we're all individuals and we have plenty of differences, but what you'll learn here applies to all of us. That's because every single one of us, at one point or another in our life will struggle with problems. There's absolutely nothing wrong with that. In fact, it's a perfectly normal part of life. What happens, though, is people often don't know how to handle difficulties in life when they inevitably darken your doorstep. This is where Emotional Core Therapy (ECT) can help you. I've been practicing it and using it to heal people, including many Christians, throughout my career. Even better, you can learn how to use it to help yourself.

Though this is not specifically a religious book, if you are a Christian you will find that ECT will become an indispensable part of your spiritual life. It is not designed as a religious practice, but it fits in perfectly with virtually all faith traditions and belief systems, as you will soon discover.

My approach to therapy is to first make sure that people realize that an anguished mind is every bit as painful (sometimes more so) than a hurting body. Of course, people feel compelled to seek medical assistance to set a broken leg or treat a sore throat. Yet, when it comes to our mind we are either embarrassed to admit that we have a problem, or confused about our treatment options.

It doesn't have to be that way. What's important is recognizing not only that you need help, but that you deserve it. Why would you deprive yourself of something that could be so beneficial to your life? In using Emotional Core Therapy, I've come to understand that there is no one "right way" to do therapy. There are lots of great therapists out there, utilizing a wide variety of highly innovative and successful techniques. We build upon the work of those who have gone before us. For example, Sigmund Freud, the founder of the discipline of psychoanalysis, is held in high regard and developed lots of useful treatment techniques. Albert Ellis, an American psychologist, brought the world Rational Emotive Behavior Therapy, which is well respected and used by many therapists. Many other great therapy approaches exist that day in and day out help people to grow and understand themselves better. If I tried to teach all of them, however, it would be overwhelming for the patient. ECT introduces a group of techniques that are simple to do, and they work over time. More importantly, it empowers people to help themselves. If I could teach someone the perfect baseball swing, but they can only do it when I am right there standing next to them, what good would that do for them? By the same token, what good is therapy if it doesn't work when you leave the therapist's office? That is a basic premise that I always keep in mind when teaching people about the power that all of us have within ourselves to release our pain and to feel better. ECT has a primary goal of autonomy for the client.

And when you think about it, isn't that very compatible with the goals of Christianity? Human beings want enlightenment, they want to live their lives with peace of mind and contentment. Christians find this by getting in touch with God through Jesus Christ, and of course even people who live a more secular lifestyle seek calmness and tranquility for their soul. That is why ECT is a truly universal approach that can benefit each and every one of us.

Emotional Core Therapy helps put structure and better performance on one's therapy by providing a simple framework. This new therapy approach examines the root cause of all emotional problems, which is entering and leaving relationships with people, places, or things. Once one feels the emotional pain of fear and loss, they start to examine their body and mind sensations. By learning to monitor their feelings, people can find out what has "hurt" them in life, and only then can they begin to heal it. Consider the following phrases:

"Once bitten, twice shy."

"Fool me once, shame on you. Fool me twice, shame on me."

"The definition of insanity is doing the same thing over and over again and expecting different results."

The Bible says, "And call upon me in the day of trouble: I will deliver thee, and thou shalt glorify me." (Psalms 50:15)

Each one of these offers advice for identifying what it is that hurts us, along with a corresponding solution that implies we grow and learn from the conflict. This is the same fundamental logic of ECT, to learn from each time that we have debilitating feelings of fear and loss. Following Jesus is all about spiritual growth and learning new things about life every day, no matter how long you have lived in this world.

Let's look at something as simple as putting on a jacket on a cold and blustery day. Most every child knows that to protect them from the cold, one has to put on layers of clothes to keep warm. It is something we all learn at a young age. This is the same dynamic we are doing with our feelings. Harmful feelings of fear and loss can cause harm and danger to one's body in much the same way that a snowy and wintry day can adversely affect a person dressed only in a T-shirt and shorts. ECT is a form of self-care that has as a desired effect to reduce toxic pain. The goal of this book is to make the reader so familiar with the process they can use it any time, just like one uses a winter jacket. At the heart of Emotional Core Therapy is learning how to identify and process the four authentic feelings that arise from all relationships. They are joy, grief, fear, and relief.

Could it get any more human than that? Moreover, if you are a Christian, you will come to see ECT as yet another component in your walk of faith. People who are into praying will be pleasantly surprised to realize that your prayer life will become much easier to pursue, and even more beneficial, when you incorporate ECT into your thinking. Of course, it will also work for those who do not practice a particular faith. Why? Because ECT is an approach that encompasses the entire human family. There is no problem in the world that someone else has not experienced. Emotional Core Therapy offers a practical, realistic and very effective method for dealing with all of them. It all begins with honoring your five senses: hearing, seeing, smelling, tasting and touching. Pay close attention to all five of them. What are they telling you? You will never really know if you impair your senses with toxins such as caffeine, drugs, or alcohol. An individual who honors his senses will be more aware not only of the outside world, but of their own inner world as well.

I like to use metaphors. They've been invaluable in forming my understanding of the world in assisting those who come to me for help. I will use them throughout this book. One of my favorites involves golf. A golfer needs to be honest with himself, and decide if their emotions on the course are helping or hurting them. For example, would an aspiring pro golfer who throws his clubs when he misses a drive, be an improved golfer if he handled his emotions properly? Can the proper understanding of emotions lower your score? How many shots does one throw away because of poorly handled emotions? Mastering the psychology of the mind is essential for any amateur or professional golfer who strives to be his best. The idea is to truly be comfortable with oneself as well as learn to identify feelings that are uncomfortable, but sometimes things get a bit more complex. Let me explain. Consider a golfer that hits four to five excellent shots in a row. To the naked eye, no problem, he is playing well, so he will want to keep the positive vibrations going. Right? Wrong, that is not what the elite golfers do! If they do, they will elevate their central nervous system, and before you know it they will make an errant shot from too much adrenaline. That is why, to the contrary, elite golfers have a calmness about them. Most have learned to maintain a good, balanced psyche. It is also important to realize that it is possible to have too many feelings of joy and relief.

For an example outside of golf, think about an adolescent listening to rock and roll music. Some teens will rock and roll for hours. They get a mindset that life is more pleasurable than it really is. That sets up an unrealistic expectation to have, i.e., that life is always that pleasurable. In reality, though, one way or another, the party will be over one day. Some kids try and use substances to keep the elevated feelings longer. The point is, you can now begin to see how having too much of the authentic feeling of "joy" can also be problematic for humans.

But this emphasis on learning how to process our true feelings and properly handle our emotions not only goes well beyond golf, it actually applies to virtually all of life. Think about it, even without a major crisis, on a day in, day out basis we all have minor psychic pain of one sort or another. It could be a difficult to live with mate, a boss with a short fuse, kids who are always "pushing your buttons," etc. Though not debilitating, these daily irritants can build up and steal away your happiness and peace of mind. As you become more aware of your feelings, you will be better able to decide what you can handle and what you cannot. It may need to involve terminating certain relationships. For example, if a boss is so overbearing that you are living in misery, the only solution might be to find a new job. But there are also other techniques that can be used for identifying and releasing feelings, as we will see.

Needless to say, you also have to use prudence and common sense too. People who trust in God will pray for the wisdom of discernment. God does provide guidance, and as you no doubt know, it can come in many different forms. ECT is a new development in your life, but new opportunities often come into your life in ways you had not previously expected. God working "in mysterious ways" is not just a cliché. Christians believe that it is truly a manifestation of God's loving providence.

Of course, if at any point you ever feel that you might be a danger to yourself or other people, you may need to call 911 or check into a hospital Emergency Room. Though common and universal to all people, normally mild ailments such as sadness, anxiety and anger can sometimes be serious enough to require hospitalization. In every situation, err on the side of caution, as it's always better to be safe than sorry.

To help explain the many benefits of Emotional Core Therapy I want for you to imagine a rudderless rowboat rowing down the river. What does it take for a rowboat to traverse down the waterway? Fuel of course. In this case, fuel would consist of a healthy diet. By that we mean not using stimulants such as coffee, caffeinated soda, and excess sugar, all of which affect the central nervous system. All stimulants or depressants affect the four authentic feelings of joy, grief, fear, and relief. Minor uses such as a cup of coffee in the morning or salt on your popcorn, likely would not affect a person's central nervous system in a chronic manner. The best advice I can give here is to speak with your family doctor, clergyperson or spiritual mentor if you have concerns with your dietary intake. The important factor to remember is that food and drink can have a positive or negative impact on your central nervous system. Although the topic of food intake is beyond the scope of this book, just keep in mind that the relationship exists.

Back to our rudderless rowboat…it's gliding through the water effortlessly and smoothly. Try and visualize the peaceful state of the rowboat as it courses downstream. Soft, tranquil, yet very sturdy. Quite a vessel, wouldn't you say? Now imagine if this rudderless rowboat was able to traverse the sea and ocean for months and years in the same manner. What an enjoyable experience. This is ideally, the emotional state of a person who has successfully learned ECT. Think of the goals of many major religions, Buddhism for example. Calming the mind through meditation is considered very important, and the feelings evoked by ECT are similar in many ways. Even if a person never read a word about ECT, they could have this same feeling. How? By just staying emotionally balanced and healthy their whole lives. Sounds like a fun and enjoyable way of life. So what is so hard about achieving this state? Rather than give you the answer, let's realistically explore what happens to people as they experience life using the rudderless rowboat example.

Now, with our rowboat traveling the waterways, what happens from time to time? Inclement weather affects our sturdy little vessel. High winds and rain, along with cold and hot weather seriously call into question the reliability of the boat to keep out water. From time to time, a big wave (rainstorm) causes water to leak into the rowboat. Consequently, the rowboat slows down and its power is weakened. If a tornado or hurricane passes in the path of the rowboat, you can be slowed to a near stop. This is in effect, what happens to individuals when the relationships they are in go sour. Their vitality and vigor for life becomes diminished when negative and toxic emotions adversely affect their central nervous system. Recall how it feels when you lose a close friend who you bonded with for several years, or any other human tragedy. The devastation that they felt is similar to what has happened to someone aboard this fictionalized boat.

Taking the analogy a step further, we could reasonably ask why not just use the rowboat in a small river and have an enjoyable boating experience for life? The problem is, that is not generally how humans operate. First of all, people need food, water, and shelter to live. This takes money and resources to provide these invaluable resources. Work has built in stresses like bosses as well as physical and emotional demands. Work requires training. This means schooling and education, which are all mandatory requirements of our youth. All of these demands will inevitably cause stress on the body and mind. Most of us (once again imagining the rowboat) will have water leak in from time to time. Faith includes finding the courage to overcome adversity when it does strike. People who trust in God lean on Him for support, just as the Bible teaches. You can look at ECT as just one other way for God to put His arms out to you in peace and love. Consider ECT as a beautiful gift from God to mankind.

Another dynamic of human nature is the needs and demands of people. Most, if not all humans will test themselves somewhat with wanting more out of life; in other words, they prefer not remaining in the small waterway. People will usually challenge themselves to achieve what they perceive the next person down the street has achieved. Whether it's new friends, lovers, work, or travel, humans find a way to partake in more and more relationships. As Emotional Core Therapy explains, it is the entering and leaving of relationships that can cause tension and stress in our lives. Examine the list below of commonly occurring stressful events in life that can cause debilitating feelings of fear and loss.

1. Death of a family member including spouse/child/sibling/etc.
2. Divorce or separation of a spouse
3. Major health problem such as cancer, diabetes, etc.
4. Being fired or placed on review at work
5. Problems or disputes with relatives or close friends
6. Pregnancy or gaining stepchildren
7. Being bullied at school
8. Failing grades at school
9. Marital affair/catching your partner cheating
10. Being relocated at work
11. Spilt or breakup of a partner/boyfriend/girlfriend
12. Changing your career or schooling plans.
13. Major weather disaster such as hurricane or tornado
14. Loss of important leisure activity due to injury
15. Being harassed at work
16. Loss of home due to moving or relocation for work
17. Long standing disagreements with spouse or family member
18. Children getting in trouble with the law
19. Change in health of close friend or family member
20. Home being foreclosed upon.
21. Problems with the law including jail/parole, etc.
22. Children going off to college/getting married
23. Stock market crash
24. Close friends move out of state/out of town
25. War/major epidemic of disease such as serious influenza lasting months

Any one of the above stressful events would cause any human being to suffer. The real difference is that emotionally healthy people, including those practicing ECT, appropriately process their feelings. Yes, many people rely on their faith to get them through times of suffering, but even the most devout acknowledge that "God helps those who help themselves."

The predominate state of a person that successfully has learned ECT is one of tranquility and a balanced equilibrium. Joy, grief, fear, or relief does not dominate an emotionally healthy person. These four authentic feelings are just temporary states that affect the person from time to time. Let's face it. A perfectly smooth running rowboat does not exist. It is not realistic. What is realistic is that one can expect some minor water coming in from time to time. In rare instances, a rushing torrent of flooding water threatens to sink the rowboat. A perfect analogy for when we need to seek out professional help. This means visits to therapists, social workers, doctors, etc.

Let me describe for you what life would look like for an emotionally healthy person practicing ECT. This person is committed to a life of having peace and comfort in their day. Their mind is allowed to daydream and reflect. Reflection is key as it is a relaxed way the mind can roam and wander from thought to thought in an effortless manner. There is no effort underway to learn and acquire information. Cognition is another word for learning. That takes effort and taxes the mind. The beautiful state of meditation is different in that the mind is not charged with working on a task. Ask anybody with a strong prayer life and they will tell you how impactful this can be, and how it can literally transform your entire outlook on life.

One way we may be able to attain a healthy meditative state would be taking a bubble bath in a dimly lit room with candles and soft music. This atmosphere allows the mind to wander. A bubble bath is not possible for everyone on a daily basis of course, but the point is nonetheless well taken. One needs to create an atmosphere of self-soothing. There is just no substitute for taking time to relax every day. It is a way of loving yourself to allow oneself time to be rested and peaceful. When you can relax you have a great opportunity to let your mind wander and daydream. Oftentimes I work with clients for a month or two just on learning the valuable state of meditation. Here is a list of 40 popular ways to relax:

1. Exercise before work, get the blood flowing
2. Practice yoga, Pilates, or chi gong
3. Reduce the amount of coffee you drink
4. Go for a run around the city at lunch time
5. Practice deep breathing throughout the day
6. Get the daily chores out of the way now instead of worrying about them
7. Cut out the sugar in your diet (it causes stress)

8. Throw out stuff around your house you really don't need or use
9. Do some gardening in the yard
10. Get some fresh air by taking a brisk nature walk
11. Practice Mindfulness
12. Do some deep muscle stretches
13. Practice sewing or needlework
14. Go somewhere where sunlight warms your face
15. Call some old friends and meet for lunch
16. Tidy your room and make your bed so it's clean when you go to sleep
17. Head down to the beach and walk in shallow water
18. Escape by reading a relaxing book
19. Take some allotted time to do nothing at all
20. Go to Red Light Tanning
21. Drink some lemon tea or green tea
22. Take a day off from work
23. Go and see a comedy show
24. Get a neck or a foot massage
25. Go for a walk around the markets or somewhere with lots of natural produce
26. Ride a bike in nature
27. Read a book you enjoyed as a child
28. Get off the computer and relax your eyes
29. Listen to classical music
30. Play any sporting event such as golf or bowling with friends for fun
31. Watch a movie or TV show

32. Say a reflective prayer over and over in a relaxed chant
33. Sing to yourself in a humming or relaxed manner
34. Journal, draw or paint your random thoughts
35. Watch your thoughts without engaging them
36. Go fishing or boating
37. Spend some time with your dog or other animal
38. Pick up a hobby you have neglected
39. Plan a getaway you would love to take in the future
40. Go out to a nice restaurant for dinner

OK, at this point, you may be saying, thanks for that great list, but really, why would someone possibly write another self-help book? After all, ECT sounds interesting, but there are many excellent psychology books out there that do a great job at highlighting specific psychology techniques. There are wonderful books on ways to improve one's individual health on a variety of mental health issues. Whether it is depression, anxiety, anger, addiction, narcissistic disorders, obsessive disorders, or the many other disorders of the self, odds are, someone has written a book on the topic. Add on couples, family, and workplace stress, and you will find more good books on ways to get one's emotional health back on track. Not to mention sacred scriptures and all kinds of books offering religious and spiritual guidance. So why add yet another book? First and foremost, people are still suffering emotional trauma day in and day out. Look at America's prison system. We have several million people incarcerated in our jails and prisons, with millions of others on probation or parole. On top of that, we have thousands of people in psychiatric hospitals. Moreover, we have millions of people who are in so much pain that they are either under a doctor's care, or are self-medicating through illegal drugs or alcohol to numb the pain. It's a gigantic national problem.

Much of this pain can be avoided with proper care of one's emotional health. That is why I think it is so important for people to learn the techniques of Emotional Core Therapy, which is the primary purpose of this book. It is a way to take care of one's self in a preventive manner. Think about all of the other self-care techniques that you employ every day. Taking a shower and brushing your teeth for example. Both of these daily habits help keep disease away. ECT is also a daily habit, that when used correctly can help maintain one's health. Even better, it is so simple that normal everyday people can practice the technique. Is it the only route to mental health? Not at all. In fact, I would love to write a psychology book using the numerous other techniques available to me as a therapist. Unfortunately, it would be just too overwhelming. Probably ten to twenty volumes long. And guess what? It still would not be complete. It also would not work. Most people would not read it, much less buy it. In most large bookstores you can find a section on ways to do things easily. For example, books with titles like, Divorce for Dummies. Taxes for Dummies. How to Build a House for Dummies. These books offer quick and easy ways, often abbreviated, to help people with specific problems. Another example would be Cliff Notes. Don't have time to read Romeo and Juliet, you can pick up a book of Cliff Notes that will simplify matters and at least give you the main idea.

While this book is not a Cliff Notes primer on psychology, it is an attempt to shorten or abbreviate one specific way to stay emotionally healthy. Nothing would make me happier than for this book to rid humanity of all of its emotional problems. Sort of like the fountain of youth, you can stay young forever. As ECT highlights, however, this is impossible! Why? Relationships, toxic or harmful, are a part of life. They are unavoidable. Even Jesus said that we will always have trouble in this world. The only thing one can really do is educate oneself on what is a healthy relationship. A healthy relationship can only begin if one is emotionally healthy. A healthy or stable person, as seen through the lens of ECT is a person who has full awareness of the four authentic feelings, joy, grief, fear, and relief. Furthermore, a healthy person knows a relaxed and meditative lifestyle.

A healthy relationship is built on mutual respect. The communication style is one of openness and honesty. Lying and stealing are not part of a healthy relationship. Being able to trust and share one's authentic feelings is paramount to a healthy relationship. One can only do this if the relationship allows for a caring atmosphere to exist where all feelings are welcomed and understood. This means that one has to be able to share feelings of fear and loss as well as joy and relief.

One of the most important benefits of Emotional Core Therapy is that you begin to examine why particular relationships cause you debilitating feelings. This enables you to learn from your relationships and make better "relationship choices" next time. You begin to empower yourself by identifying and participating in healthy relationships, which in turn leads to more hope for the future.

In order to understand ECT one has to be ready to love oneself and protect oneself. Christianity teaches this same principle, of course, so ECT becomes even more effective as you deepen your faith. By the same token, it is also remarkably effective for those without any adherence to a particular religion or spirituality. Furthermore, it is necessary to be willing to take a risk and practice something that you have not done before. This book about Emotional Core Therapy is meant as a teaching tool. That is why we used the approach of storytelling. It is a great way to teach as you can learn through others' experience in a joyful, non-threatening manner.

The alternative, simply ignoring our emotional needs or seeking relief in unhealthy ways, can prove disastrous. Oftentimes people begin to learn inappropriate self-soothing techniques and bad habits in their teens. My hope is that by writing in a short, storytelling, easy to read style, even young people can start to learn to process their feelings in a safe and healthy manner.

When we examine the escalating prevalence of mental health issues, we may ask the following question: is there a single remedy or psychological approach that works? If so, why don't we use it? Why don't we have a cure for mental health like we have for polio? The truth is we have a multiplicity of approaches that may alleviate many symptoms, but there does not exist one single approach that every therapist has utilized and every client has used and become healthy. There does not exist a one-sized fits all approach to therapy. If there did, all therapists would be trained in that approach and use it with their clients.

A similar question can be asked regarding ECT's simplistic approach. Why would ECT not work to help mental health issues? What would be problematic when one processes authentic feelings? What happens when one monitors their body for symptoms of stress and then works to alleviate those symptoms through commonly used psychological techniques? What could be problematic with the continued use of meditation and relaxation on a daily basis? What would be problematic about examining all relationships from a framework of entering and leaving them as a cause of stress? Well, the fact of the matter is that time and will (motivation) are needed for this approach to fully work. Why? Mature relationships, work, school, lover, friend, etc. frequently require the needs of others to be met. Even our own needs often have to be met in relationships. Whether it's emotional, financial, spiritual, or physical, humans are often required or asked to meet the needs of others in relationships. A key point of ECT is the concept of working to meet the needs of yourself as well as others in relationships.

As we begin to discuss the benefits of ECT we need to point out that some people may have to work longer and harder to reap these benefits. There are individuals who have impairments with one or more of their five senses (seeing, touching, smelling, tasting, and hearing). These impairments can cause their feelings of joy, grief, fear, and relief to be adversely affected. For example, a visually impaired person may not receive the same response watching a movie at the theatre as a non-visually impaired person. Also, there are individuals who have suffered severe early childhood trauma that is permanent in nature. For example, a child suffering from fetal alcohol syndrome may have some sensory problems that affect the ability to sense and feel. It is not that some of the benefits of Emotional Core Therapy will not be utilized, but the desired outcome of learning ECT may be harder than usual. Another example would be those individuals in chronic pain. I have seen several patients over the years suffer debilitating accidents that cause acute pain. When the pain is so pervasive as to effect a person's entire day, they might not be able to fully sense their feelings.

What other situations would arise that would cause ECT to not be successful? This book outlines situations and exceptions to where ECT may not have success. Like all treatment approaches people have to be comfortable with the process. Having the book told in a "simple storytelling fashion" is a means that has been successful with other psychological techniques, and I hope and trust that you will find it very helpful here as well.

If your goal is to be an authentic human being, then what would be more authentic than practicing ECT on a daily basis? What would be more authentic than respecting one's four authentic feelings? We have all heard of the book, "The Seven Habits of Highly Effective People." The book has a core premise that highly effective people all share certain key virtues, which may very well be true. Let's take this same framework for emotional health. What would the seven habits of an emotionally healthy person look like?

I believe that it would be a great habit if you were to always honor your four true feelings. Meditation is a way of caring for oneself, so that is another great habit, as is honoring the four true feelings of others. In fact, as far as emotional health is concerned, those three habits would be a great way to live. So we might even jokingly refer to ECT as, "the three habits of emotionally healthy and highly effective people."

So if you're ready to finally love yourself to the core, to love yourself enough to care for yourself emotionally in ways that will improve your life forever, keep reading. Once you begin, your life, including your Christian beliefs, prayer life and your relationship with God will never be the same. You're in for a journey that will transform the quality of your being.

All identifiable information about actual clients has been changed to protect patient confidentiality. Moreover, all the cases mentioned in this book can be assumed to be fictional. Mr. Moylan treats all of his clients, religious and secular, with the same empathy and compassion. His ECT model strives to work from each client's particular worldview. Some cases are hypothetical and are used as a teaching tool.

ECT Flow Chart

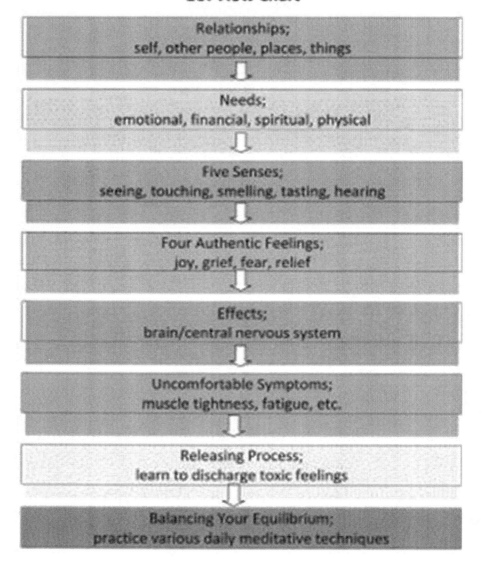

Relationships;
self, other people, places, things

⬇

Needs;
emotional, financial, spiritual, physical

⬇

Five Senses;
seeing, touching, smelling, tasting, hearing

⬇

Four Authentic Feelings;
joy, grief, fear, relief

⬇

Effects;
brain/central nervous system

⬇

Uncomfortable Symptoms;
muscle tightness, fatigue, etc.

⬇

Releasing Process;
learn to discharge toxic feelings

⬇

Balancing Your Equilibrium;
practice various daily meditative techniques

CHAPTER ONE
How ECT Works

They say that "money makes the world go round," but that's not true. Emotions do. As a matter of fact, you could easily come to the conclusion that having emotions (also called "feelings") is what distinguishes us as human beings. What's most remarkable, however, is the range of emotions. There are well over 100. I've listed below a partial list of feelings to show the varied names we use for expressing ourselves:

1. Loving
2. Wonderful
3. Joyous
4. Happy
5. Peaceful
6. Satisfied
7. Ecstatic

8. Content
9. Serene
10. Pleased
11. Elated
12. Excited
13. Overjoyed
14. Glad
15. Festive
16. Thrilled
17. Enthusiastic
18. Eager
19. Cheerful
20. Optimistic
21. Anxious
22. Fearful
23. Tormented
24. Nervous
25. Pessimistic
26. Depressed
27. Helpless
28. Disappointed
29. Upset
30. Bitter
31. Frustrated
32. Inflamed
33. Incensed
34. Tense
35. Irritated

36. Remorseful
37. Unsure
38. Rejected
39. Offended
40. Heartbroken

These emotions can literally make us ecstatically happy or depressed to the point of utter despair. It has no doubt been this way for all of human history, but today modern psychology has unlocked the secrets of how we process our emotions. Learning how to do so in healthy ways – rather than harmful – is at the heart of Emotional Core Therapy. What ECT demonstrates is that no matter how many different names you have for these hundreds of different feelings, they all can be broken down, or categorized into one of four authentic feelings. These are joy, grief, fear, or relief.

As you read this book you will come to understand that there is no single psychological technique that works for all people. That is because every individual is uniquely different and every mental health professional varies in their approach to therapy. As a matter of fact, I borrow heavily from a number of techniques from various schools of therapy to help my clients grow. For example, when I deal with addiction issues as the primary problem, I may try three or four different techniques from three to four different schools of therapy. I am not beholden to just one approach. The focus is always on the client's growth. So for an alcohol problem I may use techniques from multiple approaches such as:

1. Family Systems Therapy, which explores patterns from one's family of origin.
2. Cognitive Behavioral Therapy, which can focus on rewards and consequences to change behavior.
3. Gestalt Therapy, which uses role playing to help clients to see outside of themselves.

We won't go into detail on these other techniques. I only mention them here to make it clear that there is a plethora of legitimate and effective approaches for dealing with emotional issues. Keep in mind that in graduate school, therapists are trained in specific specialties, and I'm not here to advocate one approach over the other or to denigrate or critique others' work. As an individual, you will of course have to discover for yourself what will work best in your own life. What I do want to emphasize is that, within the multifaceted mental health world, ECT utilizes fundamentally sound psychology techniques to treat a variety of common emotional ailments within a simple and effective framework.

Today, people are becoming more and more aware of the critical role that stress plays when it comes to both our mental and physical well-being. Incredibly, we now know that stress is the number one killer of the human species. An overburdened psyche (filled with excessive fear) or a depressed psyche are not healthy for anyone long term. You simply cannot tax the central nervous system for too long without ramifications.

Yes, the link between stress and heart disease and all kinds of other diseases is well established. But the overriding question is what can we do about it? Forget the idea of completely eliminating stress from your life. That's impossible. Each new day brings with it the possibility of stressful situations. It simply comes with the territory when living in an imperfect world. There are always going to be things that we find stressful. Consider the game of golf (this is instructive regardless of whether or not you play the game yourself). Playing golf involves experiencing all four of what are termed the "four authentic feelings." These are joy, grief, fear and relief. My main focus in counseling golfers/athletes and other clients is to have them understand these four authentic feelings. Anger is a reaction to grief and is also analyzed in counseling sessions. All four affect your golf swing.

In simple terms all four true or authentic feelings evolve from entering and leaving relationships. Let's take a look at the following diagram. As you can see from this diagram, when you go towards something you like there is "Joy". What is Joy? In simple terms, it is a pleasurable state of arousal. Most people can understand this sensation if you ask them the question, "What are you most optimistic about?" Their answer will likely be directed towards a relationship they are happy about entering into. An example would be seeing your favorite sports team win a close game. Another example would be hugging a loved one or someone you admire.

Flow Chart of Four Primary Feelings

Grief is what happens when you leave a relationship that you enjoyed. For example, leaving your warm, cozy house on a rainy day. Or perhaps leaving a loved one, when you go off to work in the morning.

This diagram also shows what happens when you enter a relationship that you dislike. A relationship that you dislike will provoke feelings of fear. An example would be climbing inside a cage with a hungry lion. Or jumping into the ocean if you don't know how to swim.

When you leave a situation you dislike, there is relief. For example, escaping out of a cage in which a hungry lion had been running after you. Or reaching the shoreline after almost drowning in the ocean.

This flowchart of four authentic feelings is critical to understanding Emotional Core Therapy. Please go ahead and test the validity of the four authentic feelings by substituting several of your own relationship experiences for those that we have listed here. Try several for each authentic feeling and you will see that the flowchart is an accurate depiction of what happens to us human beings throughout the day. Stress, in the form of fear and grief will be with us our entire lives. ECT is the only therapy approach that addresses this stress openly, honestly, and accurately.

To see how the full sequence of events occurs with Emotional Core Therapy, let us now look at another diagram. This time we will examine the eight logical sequences of events that occur when authentic feelings are aroused and released. This diagram takes us from beginning to end in the ECT process.

As the ECT Flowchart below highlights, it is relationships that cause the four authentic feelings of ECT to arise. Specifically, relationships with our selves or others usually involve needs being met. For the sake of simplicity, I organize needs into four categories. These are emotional, financial, spiritual, and physical. Throughout the human lifespan humans will be challenged to get these four needs met in a satisfactory manner. Also, it will be a challenge to meet other's needs. Our five senses – hearing, touching, smelling, tasting, and seeing – are needed to help identify the four authentic feelings that arise when we enter or leave a relationship. These four authentic feelings send messages to the brain, which is part of the central nervous system. Oftentimes when one of the four authentic feelings are severe or debilitating, our body will feel uncomfortable with symptoms of stress such as muscle tightness, shaking, or fatigue.

The benefit of ECT is that it simplifies the identifying of feelings thus allowing people to be empowered with their emotional being. ECT teaches one to cathartically release these feelings in an appropriate way. Furthermore, ECT works with clients to learn and acquire a calm, meditative state of being that is free from stress. That calm and meditative state of being is the 8th and final step of the ECT process and it is fully compatible with the practices of virtually all religions. Practicing ECT can teach you how to have a peaceful, loving relationship with your God throughout the day. What Christian does not want that?

Just about every person of faith knows how to focus on thoughts and images that bring tranquility to the mind. That's because spiritual leaders have been teaching such practices for thousands of years. Now, it is also true that many belief systems have developed beautiful and often quite elaborate ceremonies, rituals, and other very precise religious activities. The idea of ECT is certainly not to discourage any of that. At the proper time and place these traditions are indeed appropriate and they bring much meaning and joy to people's lives. However, when using ECT all you have to do is simply focus on those aspects of your faith that emphasize peaceful, loving imagery. You do not have to be rigid or formulaic in any way. There is no need to exert any effort at all, or to try to recite specific words or rituals while praying. This may differ in the particulars from one faith tradition to the other, but the goal is the same: to quiet the mind and to enter a serene state where daydreaming and reflection come to us in a way that feels natural and spiritually nourishing. This is how ECT bridges the gap between psychology and religion.

By using the ECT flowchart, adherents of every religion, as well as non-religious people, will be able to process their emotions in a healthy manner that reaps enormous benefits in their everyday life. For those who consider themselves religious or spiritual, ECT will strengthen their faith while at the same time this technique allows future authentic feelings to be more easily identified and processed. I would suggest that you review the ECT flowchart and examine the eight concepts that demonstrate the ECT process from beginning to end. After studying the ECT flowchart several times, try and envision a particularly traumatic event in your life. Did your experience resemble the sequence highlighted in the ECT flowchart? If so, how did your experience mirror that of ECT? If not, do not worry. We have the entire book to help you learn the ECT process.

ECT Flow Chart

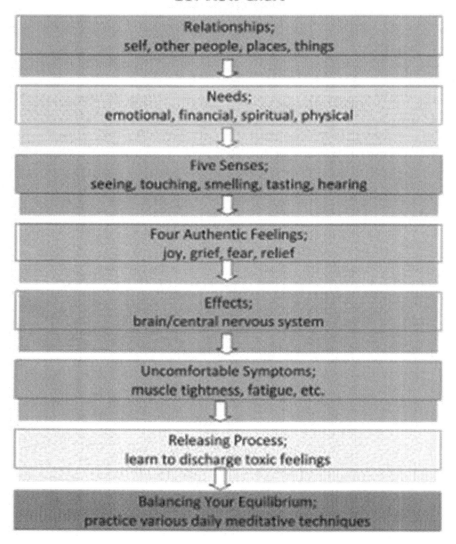

When you enter a relationship that you like there is joy (this is not limited to relationships with other people, as it could be many things; think of eating your favorite ice cream). When you leave something that you like there is grief (saying good-bye to someone you love). When you go towards something you dislike there is fear. Imagine walking near a snake pit. When you leave a fearful event, there is relief. Ask any golfer and they will tell you that playing golf is in itself a relationship – a relationship with nature. The tougher the golf course, the tougher the test is emotionally on a golfer's psyche.

Grief (otherwise known as loss) and fear (otherwise known as anxiety) are the two most debilitating feelings that golfers face when they play. Unfortunately, for most amateurs every round of golf is filled with these unwanted feelings. Golfers of every level need to get a handle on their emotions each time they play – or face the consequences.

Hopefully, this is all starting to make sense to you. Yet, you very well might be asking, "Well, that's great for problems on the golf course…but what about everything else in life?" My answer: ECT does indeed pertain to every area of our life. We all need to find healthy ways to process our emotions every single day, wherever we are and whatever we are doing. It doesn't matter how old you are, your financial circumstances, your love life or anything else. Your emotions are always there. They are an integral part of who you are. It makes no sense to try to bury them or to ignore them. Even if you could, you wouldn't want to, as it would be a shallow existence to live in a world without feelings. Some people try, through drugs, alcohol and countless other means – and they often fail and end up harming themselves even more. That's precisely why it is so vital to learn how to best cope with toxic/debilitating feelings. Think of ECT as a lifestyle choice that will improve your mental health.

Like any lifestyle change, what you learn through ECT will not take root overnight, but over the course of months or years. It has to become integrated into your life. Let's take a closer look at how one's memory works. Most emotionally healthy people do various stages of Emotional Core Therapy without much thought given to the process. However, for ECT to be of true value throughout one's life, it is imperative to learn the process completely. The goal is to never forget the process of how emotions work. We spend a year in high school learning Algebra, which many of us forget a few years later. That's OK if we go on to careers that never require Algebra. But we will always have emotions! So why not learn a process of emotional healing that will serve us our entire lives no matter where we live or what we do?

All of us humans know our dates of birth, our race, ethnicity, religion, etc. Why? We know these facts about ourselves because we learned them over and over again when were young. We also were required to know these facts about ourselves at various times in our adult lives. It takes time and energy to learn these important pieces of information about our life. This information is useful and necessary as it serves to ground and center us as human beings.

ECT is also an approach that will allow you to be centered in life. As ECT explains, grief and fear are an inevitable part of life. In any given year it is likely that one in five people will incur a debilitating experience emotionally. Why not equip yourself for something so common in life? In order for one to gain use of the ECT process we are placing an ECT Flowchart at the beginning of the book and at the end of each chapter as a reference point. This allows you to gauge how much you have learned about ECT after reading a chapter. A checkpoint of key ECT issues lets you focus on key concepts at a leisurely pace.

Remember to be kind to yourself and allow yourself ample time to read the entire book. It takes time to reflect on your own experiences as well those of others. If you were going to teach a child the ABC song, how would you do it? Would you be compassionate? Supportive? Would you give treats and rewards to the child when they learn portions of the song? Why not do the same for yourself when you learn ECT? Why not be kind and supportive and reward yourself for learning something as important as protecting your own mind?

The crucial point to remember is that the process of learning ECT is easier than it looks. In fact, many of us use some of the various steps of ECT without even knowing it! For example, most people use their five senses hundreds of times a day. Most people are bombarded by other's needs (emotional, financial, spiritual, physical) throughout the day. Also, most people have messages or information sent to their central nervous system throughout the day.

Consider the book, "The Seven Habits of Highly Effective People". This widely successful book was read by millions of people throughout the world. Why was it so successful? It taught seven core principles that helped people achieve their goals. If millions of readers can learn these seven habits, why can't one learn the six major steps to ECT?

Remember, the ECT flowchart highlights eight concepts that typically occur in a relationship to cause us duress. The real work of this book is to understand five or six major concepts (understanding relationships and their needs, authentic feelings, mind and body distress, releasing feelings, and dutiful meditation). Two other concepts (learning how our five senses work and understanding how the central nervous system is affected) occur quite quickly and without much thinking. This book will only touch briefly on the two remaining parts of the ECT flowchart that occur rapidly to all of us on a daily basis.

Part of the overall ECT process we do instinctively anyway! For example, we enter and leave relationships all day long. So this is really not all that difficult for us to understand and follow. If you allow yourself the time to learn ECT, and are willing to commit the process to memory, be prepared to enjoy greater vitality and vigor. You are learning a process that will increase your enthusiasm and appreciation for life.

In order for ECT to be of real value, you need to be able to incorporate and apply the contents of this book into your day to day life. This can only occur when the ECT technique is learned and committed to one's long term memory, which only happens through repetitious work. In other words, practice, practice, practice. Over time you will enter the various steps into your short term memory. After repeated use, ECT will eventually become lodged into one's long term memory.

How Memory Works

Once a person has the technique in their long term memory, the process is learned and available for use. If you still have trouble understanding how memory works, think of remembering a ten-digit phone number. Usually it takes several tries to learn a long phone number. The ECT process requires that one monitor his mind and body for feelings and muscle response. This effort takes time to learn correctly. As you become aware of all four feelings, and their effect on you, rest assured you will start to become more emotionally balanced. In this book I will be using practical examples and cases where ECT can and would be utilized. By processing the various scenarios facing everyday common folks, you will begin to commit the approach to your long term memory. As you become more aware of all four feelings, and their effect on you, rest assured that you will become more balanced.

To help you understand ECT, let's examine how the four feelings are processed. It is our senses – seeing, touching, smelling, tasting, and hearing – that process of all of our feelings. When an individual can sense fear (such as your boss yelling at you) a message is sent to the brain, which is part of the central nervous system. The central nervous system in turn transmits messages to the muscles throughout the body. This same dynamic happens throughout the day to all of us in various degrees whenever we sense fear.

As a therapist, my theoretical orientation is described as technically eclectic. This means I use a variety of psychological techniques from a variety of schools of therapy. Over the years I have found that focusing on the release of authentic feelings has been helpful for client's growth and development. Much like getting caught in a thunderstorm, the vast majority of people get overwhelmed by emotions and lunge for the nearest umbrella. ECT, when practiced effectively, can downgrade a severe thunderstorm to just some minor drizzle. Emotional Core Therapy is effective because it filters out ambiguous words and negative thoughts by emphasizing and understanding the four true and authentic feelings.

It all begins with learning to continually monitor the four feelings. We all embark on the process at a different point in life. In my years of using ECT, I've had clients who have come to me at various stages of growth. Some are very emotionally healthy and need just a few sessions to get back on track. Others may need help in only one or two areas of life. I have empathy and compassion for all of them regardless of the stage of life they are in. This approach offers hope even for those who have suffered the worst possible cases of trauma and abuse.

Traumatic and stressful events, as most everybody unfortunately knows, come in a wide variety of shapes and sizes. The good news is that ECT is a helpful treatment option because of its inherent ability to authentically assess your problems in a simple, yet effective manner.

The goal of Emotional Core Therapy is to get clients to be as peaceful and emotionally centered as a healthy two-year old. The definition of having a peaceful, relaxing, and meditative state is to feel non-threatened, or effected, by the four authentic feelings. In other words, to have a relaxed and calm central nervous system. Envision an infant in a crib, smiling and relaxed. Just as an infant can sit in a crib in a blissful state, an adult can also achieve a calm and relaxed state of being. As you read this book you will learn techniques to achieve meditation throughout the day. Meditation, a calm state of being, is essential for people desiring to use Emotional Core Therapy. Once you learn and can comfortably practice a "calm, relaxed, sense of self, it becomes easier to identify the four authentic feelings.

Most people suffering from grief or fear (which, as we said, is also known as anxiety) come to my office in a sad state of affairs with little hope of feeling better. One technique I use is to have them reflect on a peaceful state of mind that they had sometime as a child. It may have been at school, on a beach, with a friend, etc. I then help the client realize that he can get back to that proper state of mind through utilizing many of my therapy techniques. This book will cover many of the most effective psychology techniques known to release feelings.

Of course, none of this is to imply that we're dealing with childish problems, or even trying to trace the problems back to childhood. Instead, Emotional Core Therapy teaches techniques to help yourself to learn how to process emotions properly, and in ways that are healthy rather than destructive. Remember that the four authentic feelings ultimately all stem from either entering or leaving relationships. Take, for example, a man and a woman who are having a strained relationship. Basically, their problem is "working on the marriage." Marriage is a lot of work, as each partner has to learn about the other partner's needs. In marriage counseling, I often make a list of what the husband and wife need emotionally, financially, physically, and spiritually. Both have to grow and learn about each other. With Emotional Core Therapy, we pay attention to how each feels in the relationship. The wife (Sally) in this scenario tells the therapist, "I get scared when John comes home from work. I know John works hard at his construction job during the day. His working conditions are horrible as he has to deal with all the inclement weather and a mean and demanding boss! Still, I cringe when he comes through the door in his foul moods every day."

With ECT, we focus on the meaning of her feelings. In this case, both words she uses, "scared" and "cringe" are different vocabulary names for the authentic feeling, "Fear".

What Sally is saying is that this relationship she has entered into brings fear into her life from time to time. The wife is not saying she has a terrible marriage. She just wants to address her relationship with her husband and work towards a better resolution in this particular situation.

With Emotional Core Therapy, there is a primary belief that no one deserves to live life with unwanted and toxic feelings. Furthermore, ECT has at its core a belief that withheld or internalized feelings are harmful for anyone in the long term. ECT utilizes a wide variety of commonly known techniques to release feelings. One of the most common techniques out there is to "verbalize" one's feelings. By talking out your fears with a compassionate therapist, toxic feelings such as fear (otherwise known as anxiety) are released. This is called catharsis. Catharsis is the cleansing of the soul. With

ECT, we are vigilant about cleansing our soul. Just like a young child learns to brush their teeth and wash their hands as a daily habit, your soul also needs this type of positive treatment.

There are other ways that Sally can learn to cleanse her soul. She can journal, listen to music, exercise, meditate, etc. Throughout the book you will find examples of releasing techniques. If the wife comes in with lots of complaints of fear/anxiety because she is afraid to confront her husband for not listening to her, I may focus on her learning to be more assertive with her needs. In this example, the first step is identifying the fear.

This is similar to a golfer who says that he has a panic attack every time he has to hit out of a sand bunker. He has excess fear, which adversely affects his central nervous system, and in turn this change in temperament adversely affects his golf swing. Why? The golf swing needs to be free of tension and smooth to be effective. It needs to be able to be repeated over and over in a calm manner. When a golfer lets his feelings have a negative effect on his swing it is called "choking". In other words, his nerves get in his way. A golfer will utilize a swing coach and perhaps a golf psychologist to help him through his emotional problem. Both the swing coach and golf psychologist will be supportive, caring, and allow an environment for the golfer to take risks, and to make changes with his swing. If the golfer feels excessive fear in part of his game, he needs to trust his coach to get him better. Do you see how this is similar to a woman suffering fear from her husband? That's precisely why, when I use Emotional Core Therapy I encourage clients to take risks and make changes if they are suffering debilitating feelings of fear and loss.

Another example might involve an angry father of two young boys who works a lot. He comes to therapy to get some parenting skills. He tells me, "I am overwhelmed by these two boys and hate that I sometimes yell or get angry at them." Clearly, he chose his words carefully. The young father used the word "overwhelmed" because the reality is that he has too much fear! He's fearful (worried, concerned...feel free to add your own) that he will "fail" to fully or adequately complete all of the many tasks and responsibilities expected of him based on his circumstances and position in life. The solution, then, is that he needs to be organized and structured in such a way so that he can feel a sense of accomplishment with these necessary parenting tasks.

This young man's name is Jesse and he was born and raised in rural Alabama in a family with strong Christian values. His parents always taught him that as the head of his household he would be expected to provide leadership. They based this belief on the teachings of the Bible. Jesse was honored by this responsibility, but the weight of it at times felt like it was too much for him. What would his parents think of him if they knew the inner struggle he was experiencing? The last thing he would ever want would be to disappoint them.

And he certainly did not want to disappoint God. From childhood he had been taught that as a Christian he should not live by the standards of the world, but instead by Christ's example. Jesse also wondered if he would ever be able to measure up and be the kind of ideal dad that he considered his own earthly father, the proud patriarch of a large family. These thoughts kept him awake at night and restless during the day, even when he knew he needed to be concentrating on his duties at work.

All of us adults can relate to this father as we all get overwhelmed from time to time. The dictionary definition of "overwhelming" is overpowering in effect or strength. Let's consider what is really happening to this young man in terms of the four authentic feelings. Without a doubt, he is moving towards someone or something he does not like. Let me be clear, I am not saying that he does not like his children. In fact, part of his fear is that, because he loves them so much, he's desperately afraid of failing them and his wife and his own parents. He fears that he might not be up to the task, however, because it includes so many things that worry him. For example, he may love to ride bicycles with his two children. But then the two boys invite their two friends, meaning Dad is now responsible for four kids. What then happens if they ride their bicycles near a busy street? The situation, he fears, could very easily spin out of control. What was once manageable and enjoyable, is now overwhelming.

Emotional Core Therapy will help this young father by isolating the problem, assessing the cause, and providing appropriate relief. We see that additional fear creeps into his thinking about this new activity as more children are involved, and in a more dangerous situation. When you have too much fear, it's important to reduce it somehow, if possible. A beneficial approach may be to highlight the new tasks and responsibilities involved in the four children scenario. By focusing on how Jesse feels (muscle tension, lack of sleep, headaches, etc.) we can get him to modify his activities with his children.

Moreover, as a man of deep religious convictions, Jesse can use his daily prayers as a way to relax his mind. By concentrating his spiritual energies on God, Jesse is no longer putting all of the focus (and therefore all of the burden) on himself for everything that happens in his life. ECT helps put him into a very quiet mindset where he can then process his feelings in effective and healthy ways.

The Bible teaches God's followers to lay their burdens on Him (Psalm 55:22), and Jesse was learning how to do that more and more every day. One of the key tenets of Christianity is that all things are in God's control. Therefore, by committing himself and his family to serving God (as Joshua did in the Old Testament), Jesse will bring peace to both his heart and to his mind. He was pleased to discover that such reliance on God fits in perfectly with ECT, because both are helping Jesse to release the fear and tension that he had previously allowed to rule over his life. This new mindset allows him to focus more sharply on God's loving and merciful plan for him and for the world.

In the future, once Jesse learns more about ECT, he will be able to utilize it along with prayer in other fearful, stress-inducing situations. Examples might be when he feels too much fear at work, or in other relationships. The point is, once you learn the techniques for processing your four authentic feelings, you will be amazed at how much this knowledge makes fundamental differences (for the better) in your everyday life and in the "big issues" (family, health, relationships, finances, etc.). When I speak of "big issues" I mean "life events". Emotional Core Therapy has the ability, when used correctly, to alter one's outlook, for the better, on life.

Remember earlier in this chapter we used the analogy of a thunderstorm versus drizzle to compare how one can feel less overwhelmed when using ECT? We utilize a similar framework for understanding life events. There exist hundreds, if not thousands of life events that can adversely affect the human psyche. Death, divorce, job loss, financial loss are just a few problematic life events. With Emotional Core Therapy we are compartmentalizing all of these life events into two categories: entering and leaving relationships. Emotional stress is caused by moving towards or away from a relationship you have with a person, place, or thing.

This represents a crucial step in ECT, because once you can categorize all of your life events into two categories instead of two hundred, or two thousand, you gain control over the stress. You empower yourself by recognizing that the event is separate from you. You gain confidence that this event is something you chose in your life, and (if you want to) you can leave it, by properly processing your feelings.

Let's look at a particularly stressful event in this manner. A young woman named Linda has just accepted a job offer in an adjacent state. Once she starts her new position, she discovers that her boss is a lunatic. She knows that she cannot work in this position very long without undue psychological stress. By utilizing Emotional Core Therapy, she recognizes that she has entered into a new relationship with someone. In this case, a new boss. She also recognizes that she has entered into a new relationship with a new community as the position is out of state and she is not familiar with her surroundings. Although she has a great deal of fear related to her current life predicament, she feels confident deep down. Why? Linda recognizes that she is not the problem. Yes, she will have to grieve the loss of moving, getting a new job, etc. Yet, she knows deep down that these feelings will pass. She recognizes that she can process these feelings appropriately through the various techniques that she has learned in her counseling. Utilizing ECT can allow for this very difficult life event to be manageable for this young lady.

In Linda's case, in addition to ECT, she has her religious faith to lean upon. She has been a devout Catholic her entire life, she was taught by the nuns in parochial school and hardly ever misses Sunday mass. So when she moved to this new town, one of the first things that she did was to find her new local parish. She introduced herself to the priest and after attending mass for a few weeks she volunteered to join the church choir. Music always had a way of calming her nerves and putting her into a more serene state of mind. This outlet, of course, would be available to Christians of all denominations.

These activities made Linda feel less alone in her new surroundings. She gained a renewed sense of community knowing that she could develop new relationships with people who shared her same beliefs and came from the same religious background.

Linda also joined a women's group that prayed the Rosary once a week as part of a devotion to the Blessed Mother. However, the precise words of the prayers were not her focus. Instead, in her mind's eye she would visualize a statue of Mary holding the Baby Jesus that her mother had given her as a gift upon her Confirmation. Growing up, just looking at that divine statue always brought feelings of love and tranquility to Linda's heart. Now, as she learned more and more about ECT she was discovering how such imagery, even by evoking it just by closing her eyes and using her imagination, could easily transition her into a calm and very pleasant state of mind.

Having always felt the love and protection of the Virgin Mary her entire life, this practice, along with ECT, helped Linda to make the many adjustments necessary in order to transition more smoothly into this new stage of her life and career. The craziness of her boss became less and less dreadful for Linda as she built up her faith and her confidence week after week.

Christians from other churches might use similar but somewhat different approaches. For example, setting aside quiet time in a private place for silent prayer. Not reciting exact words, but letting the mind concentrate on peaceful circumstances when the presence of Jesus was particularly powerful and imminent in your life. Serene imagery of the holiness that was enlightening your life at that special time should be the primary focus of your mind's eye.

Let's look at how our simplistic approach using Emotional Core Therapy works in a different analogy. There are two teachers caring for two groups of children in a schoolyard. One teacher supervises four children. The other teacher supervises 150. Who has the easier job? The one who is watching only four children of course! Why? Less responsibility, less tasks, less energy. That is in essence why ECT can be most beneficial to people desiring to master the mind. It simplifies emotions so they become much more manageable to handle.

We are now ready to begin to explore the most commonly occurring emotional stresses in the life span of every human being. In the upcoming chapters we will examine hypothetical as well as portions of actual cases where ECT can and has proven to be effective. As you read the various scenarios unfolding before your eyes, you can finally begin to learn the benefits of Emotional Core Therapy. In my work as a therapist, the most common psychological issues I see are depression, anxiety/fear issues. Most of these stresses to our equilibrium occur when we are with family, friends, at work, school, or in a relationship with a partner such as marriage. I will examine how ECT can help people from most walks of life. As you become more and more acclimated to the ECT process, you will begin the healthy journey back home to yourself. Think of the movie, "The Wizard of Oz." The main character, Dorothy, relates to the "Good Witch of the North" at the end of the film, repeating over and over, "There is no place like home." This reassuring chant allows her to leave the fantasy world of Oz and return home to Kansas. This is the mantra that you need to learn to fully comprehend Emotional Core Therapy. Every person is lovable. Every person deserves peace. Every person can overcome their troubled emotional state.

Keep in mind that Emotional Core Therapy works if you allow the process to work. If you are willing to make a genuine effort to grow and develop as a human being, what you read in the following pages will be transformational in your life. Over time, ECT empowers the client by giving them the confidence that they can overcome many of the major traumatic events in life. There is simply no cure for the emotional trauma that life throws at us from time to time. From hurricanes, floods, financial losses, and the loss of human life, we are all tested from time to time. It is how we respond to these hurtful events that define us as human beings. ECT instills in the client a therapy approach that strengthens the mind and helps protect the spirit of the individual.

List Five Alternative Words Used To Describe The Feeling Of "Joy"

A) GLAD

B) HAPPY

1)

2)

3)

4)

5)

NOTES:

List Five Alternative Words To Describe The Feeling Of "Grief"

A) DEPRESSED

B) SAD

1)

2)

3)

4)

5)

NOTES:

List Five Alternative Words To Describe The Feeling Of "Fear"

A) ANXIETY

B) DREAD

1)

2)

3)

4)

5)

NOTES:

List Five Alternative Words Used To Describe The Feeling "Relief"

A) RELAXED

B) REPRIEVE

1)

2)

3)

4)

5)

NOTES:

List Five Stressful Relationships (People, Places, Or Things) In Your Life

A) JOB CHANGE

B) FRIEND GETTING SICK OR ILL

1)

2)

3)

4)

5)

NOTES:

List Five Ways You Can Relax In A Meditative State

A) SWIMMING

B) KNITTING

1)

2)

3)

4)

5)

NOTES:

CHAPTER TWO
Using ECT to Treat Depression

We all hear a lot about depression these days. While not too long ago people didn't talk about it very much (other than songs about "feeling the blues"), recently there has been widespread recognition that depression is a real problem that affects millions. In fact, at some time or another, all of us feel depressed. It's just a part of life. The reasons for it are too numerous to mention. But the good news is, Emotional Core Therapy offers realistic, creative solutions for those who find it difficult to escape depression's grip.

Consider what might be a "worst case" kind of depression scenario. We all remember the catastrophic tsunami in Japan, and all of the misery that it brought to so many people. Imagine the case of a forty-year old woman in Japan. When the tsunami swept over her town, her husband died, she lost a child and her community was devastated. All of her money was lost. Now if ever there were cause for depression, this would be it. What could help this woman? Would she suffer for the rest of her life? How could she possibly recover?

I bring up an extreme example like this to challenge our thought processes. Why? The truth is, every month and every year people do survive and recover from tragedies such as this throughout the world. They even overcome these seemingly insurmountable troubles without the benefit of ECT or any other therapy for that matter. How do they do it? All it really takes is time and will for things to get better if one appropriately allows the normal occurrence of processing feelings to take place. With ECT, people are taught that all of us have the power to overcome any loss or devastation that life may throw at us. Yet, we also need to recognize that there are different levels of difficulty with whatever problems we may be facing (depression, anxiety, etc.) That is why it is important to try to rate the level of mental pain that a person is suffering. If we use a scale of one to ten, one would be when a person has virtually no problem at all, while at the opposite end of the spectrum ten would be when the problem seems almost unbearable. When there is an extremely serious problem, especially with something like depression, if it is a ten that person may need to seek immediate help in a hospital Emergency Room. However, for more moderate ailments, say a four, five, six, seven or eight, an approach such as using Emotional Core Therapy could be very beneficial.

Time and therapy are an incredibly powerful combination. Of course, it requires trust on the part of the client, and both client and therapist must view themselves as partners in the therapy process. This in turn gives power to the client. How better to give power to the client than have the client become their own therapist?

One of the most important things that we do is to identify the relationships that would benefit the client, like loved ones, friends, etc. What would be required to help them? For starters, often just being with a therapist helps, which is why the therapist needs to be accessible at various hours. Atmosphere makes a big difference too, so the office should have a kind and sincere ambience. It should also be remembered that grief does not always get resolved quickly. Trying to rush things would be counterproductive, which is why therapists always allow the unpacking of feelings to occur at its own pace.

There is, however, one big obstacle that too often gets in the way before the process can even begin. Human beings have a propensity to spend countless hours and far too much energy running away from debilitating feelings of fear and grief. But they are running in the exact opposite direction. In ECT, the goal is not to avoid our feelings, but to learn from them. For example, a very talented teenager twists her ankle doing a back flip in gymnastics practice. She is so traumatized by the pain that she is shaken to the core with fear and decides to quit the gymnastics team. Think how much better off she would be if she analyzed her feelings rather than attempting to bury them. Instead of hanging up her shoes and ending her career, she could ask her coach, "How did I land improperly? What caused the injury? What can I do to prevent it from happening again?" If she had learned Emotional Core Therapy, she would have understood how to respect her authentic feelings of fear, and then release it by discovering how to improve her technique, rather than quitting the sport.

How can she do this (respect her authentic feelings)? By learning how to monitor her own body and the signals that it is constantly providing to her. That is a crucial facet of ECT, and it can in fact be transferred to all kinds of situations in life. The releasing of feelings can involve any loss in life, or any fearful event. Since we are all unique, none of us will release our feelings in the exact same way. It's a bit of a discovery process. For example, I had one client who had a maid who would come by to clean his house. He would then have long conversations with her. She had four kids, and she would tell him about her problems and how she dealt with him. Having five children of his own, this turned out to be something that they shared in common and just talking with this woman helped him to release his feelings.

A different client, in this case an iron worker, would release his feelings on the massage table while carrying on a conversation with his massage therapist. The point is, releasing feelings is a very natural process, and often takes place in unexpected places and usually unintentionally. It does not by any means always have to take place in a therapist's office.

Another example could involve a young, shy 19-year old male. He falls head over heels for a girl at his community college.

Sadly, after three months of intense dating, she abruptly breaks up with him. Emotionally devastated, he withdraws into a shell and does not date for four years. Now ask yourself, wouldn't it have been much more emotionally healthy for this young man to instead honor his pain of grief/loss? I believe yes! Rather than stop dating women, he needs to accept the experience and view it as part of a learning process. Easy? No, not by a long shot. It takes time (often months and even years) to understand one's feelings, which is why it is a continual learning process to learn ECT. But the benefits are real and often life-changing, as in this case where the young man could start dating again within a year or so of his loss, rather than languishing in turmoil and unresolved grief for at least four years.

As these examples illustrate, we can learn a lot by examining various real life scenarios of individuals struggling with the stresses of life, which is precisely the approach of the rest of this book. The goal is to help people learn how to cope effectively with debilitating feelings. Often times I see clients have "breakthrough" moments in therapy when they realize they can control entering and leaving relationships. Clients feel empowered by seeing that the relationships they enter are of their own choosing. Furthermore, these relationships will invoke one of the four authentic feelings to occur. All my clients tell me they would rather experience the feelings of joy versus fear or grief. It is helpful for clients to then work towards joyful relationships. Let's go back to our analogy of a rowboat. Why would a rowboat choose rocky waters? Why would a person want fear and grief in their life? When I work with my clients to empower themselves to make healthy choices they become more confident.

Of course, the best way to learn something of value is to experience it oneself – but that is not always practical, not to mention desirable. For example, have someone go to the bank and withdraw all of their money. Then the person would take their life savings and burn it in an incinerator. Sure, that would most definitely cause tremendous grief and fear. We would then be able to demonstrate how processing the four authentic feelings of ECT would help the person suffering this financial loss. But since pursuing such a reckless path would be completely illogical, the next best thing is to share the success stories of people just like you and me who have very effectively used ECT to recover from emotional trauma. One of the primary purposes of this book is to demonstrate several psychological techniques in a fun and relaxed manner. It can be quite a comforting process when we identify with the experiences of others.

At its core, ECT involves externalizing one's feelings rather than internalizing them. There is a time and a place for releasing cathartic feelings, and common sense must be used. What we are trying to do is to get our feelings outside of us, and this is a process that takes time, like learning to ride a bike or to swim. For example, imagine if you lost $50,000 in some kind of financial scam. Do you think that you would just bounce back from something like that overnight? Of course not. The feelings of anger and loss would be all too genuine, and properly releasing them would not come quickly.

On the other hand, however, it would be quite regrettable to put this off too long, which would be very unhealthy for both your mind and body. Toxic beliefs, if internalized, can cause unnecessary stress and damage to the body. This in turn leads to body function problems such as muscle tightness, hand sweating and trembling. Don't underestimate the seriousness of this. A person who is under stress all of the time is risking damage to their organs, which is of course extremely hazardous.

Let's look at the example of an insurance representative who came for therapy because she found that she was in a depressed state. In fact, this woman, Tina (like all examples in this book, a fictionalized name is being used to protect this individual's identity and privacy), was suffering from major states of depression such as agitation, bad mood, no joy, trouble sleeping, lack of energy, and feeling useless. I approached her as I do all of my patients, with a goal of recovery. Both of her parents had passed away, and she had made a decision a long time ago to have children to have more support and companionship in her life. Over the course of twenty years she dutifully raised her four children, while her husband, a successful lawyer, worked tirelessly at the office.

Unbeknownst to Tina, her husband had an affair with the office secretary. Later on, he pursued another affair for an even greater length of time. Soon, he and Tina began to live separate lives under the same roof. They slept in separate bedrooms, and only conversed when issues of the home or children came up.

When Tina came to my office her level of depression was about an eight or nine. She was already under a psychiatric doctor's care for depression. She found that the prescription medications she was taking took the edge off her feelings, but still did not change her despairing outlook on life. Tina came to me with complaints of being "unloved, unwanted, lonely, sad, tired," and crying a great deal. It was not difficult to assess her problem as too much grief or loss. Too much grief or loss is another name for depression. Tina also had several bodily symptoms including lack of sleep, trouble eating and feeling fatigued. In short, the hopelessness that she felt was so bad that it negatively affected her central nervous system.

Using Emotional Core Therapy, we started to reframe some of her thinking. She began to recognize that most of her thoughts were due to leaving a long-term relationship. In this case, her husband of twenty years. Her overwhelming feelings of psychic pain began to lessen over time as she learned to isolate the problem. As she became more and more aware of the four authentic feelings, she recognized that she had too much grief in her life. Over the course of eight to ten months, she began to release her feelings both in therapy and in her daily life. Every client is unique. I often have to try several different techniques before we have success in releasing feelings of grief. In Tina's case we had great success using psychology techniques that involved role playing. I would pretend to be the husband and we would reenact some of the situations that caused her emotional pain. By doing this in a nonthreatening environment of the counseling office, Tina was able to finally express herself properly. She was finally able to release her psychic pain. Another technique we used was to have Tina talk to an empty chair. The empty chair was a nonthreatening way for Tina to get her anger (otherwise known as a reaction to grief) out of her mind and body. Sometimes the pretend person in the chair was her husband. Sometimes we had Tina talk to her "pretend self" using the empty chair technique. By having Tina approach herself in a kind manner she began to have compassion and empathy for herself. Tina learned to be kind to herself by using healthy and upbeat language to address to herself how she was feeling.

Moreover, during this time Tina rekindled an in interest in following Jesus that she had begun back in college but had never developed as fully as she had once intended. Having grown up in a family where faith never played any role, she was now coming to understand what an important role belief in Jesus as her Lord and Savior could play in helping to treat her depression. Prayer and meditation are key concepts in Christianity, and as Tina studied more about the religion, she felt drawn toward practicing daily Bible reading. By concentrating her thoughts on the meaning of the Scriptures, her mind remained in the present moment rather than letting fear and depressing thoughts pre-occupy her thinking. It was an excellent fit with the approach and goals of ECT that Tina was learning. In fact, the more she learned about ECT, the more she came to understand that such reflective Bible reading could be an important addition to her toolbox of techniques that she was compiling for finally dealing properly with her depression issues.

Tina would sit in a comfortable chair and begin by reciting a small prayer. If her thoughts would begin to wander, she would briefly stop reading, take a few slow, deep breaths, and then resume. This brought about the desired effect of bringing stillness and quietude to her mind. It put her into a mental state that was focused on God and therefore detached from distracting thoughts of self-criticism or feelings of being hurt by the past actions of others. This helped Tina to process her emotions in a much healthier way, just as she was discovering by learning and using the ECT process.

There are also many other ways to achieve these desired results. For example, Tina would practice mindfulness, a highly effective technique to calm the central nervous system down, by doing yoga in her living room after her prayer time. Mindfulness is an effective method of not worrying about the future or dwelling on the past, but simply focusing one's attention on the present moment. Studies have shown that mindfulness has positive effects on both people's mental and physical health.

Most of my clients learn 5-10 good relaxation techniques like prayer and mindfulness that they can use daily. Over the years, I have seen clients make better decisions when they have a calmer state of being. ECT strives to work from a client's perspective so with each new client we research their history. We try to find what has worked in the past and what each client is comfortable in doing as a meditation exercise. As a reminder, a meditative lifestyle and state of being, is the eighth step of the ECT Flowchart. We may not always be able to achieve this goal on a day to day basis, but the more we make an effort to stay calm and relaxed and make mental health a priority in life, the better chance we have of identifying stress.

Tina also had a marvelous sense of humor so we used humor on a number of occasions to release toxic feelings of loss. She would often joke about what it was like to be in a dead end relationship. For example, she'd say, "Being in a dead relationship is like having a dead horse in your living room." She would then pretend she had a horse lying around in the house. Tina was able to cathartically release psychic pain by using humor to let go of unwanted feelings of loss.

Another way that Tina and I were able to combat her depression was by working to bring more joy into her life. We made a list of twenty attributes that she liked about herself. As we discussed this list of twenty joyful characteristics a main theme continued to pop up. Tina was a very good and devoted mother to her four children. She was especially happy to read the Bible verse that said: "But women will be saved through childbearing, assuming they continue to live in faith, love, holiness, and modesty." (I Timothy 2:15) Over the course of therapy of under a year, we highlighted how Tina was able to bring joy to her children's life, and in turn to her own. She also started to do things that brought her joy herself. For example, she began to power walk for exercise and stress reduction, along with making new friends who were much more respectful of her needs. Tina was able to reduce her level of depression from a seven or eight level to a three to five level over the course of our therapy, which utilized some ECT techniques.

Tina chose to stay married for the next few years to provide stability for her youngest child to go off to college. This meant that she had to sacrifice her own needs and wants. Whenever one sacrifices something, there exists a chance for grief. Years later, Tina came by to see me and she looked much better. She finally was able to get her own needs met as her husband moved out of the house.

Prescription medications numbed Tina's pain but did little to change her underlying condition of a poor relationship. She began to decrease her medication as she saw it as a form of escape or addiction to be on three to four medications. Accordingly, she was able to reduce her prescribed medications to just one anxiety tablet versus three to four. Thus, Tina was able to reduce her self-described addiction to prescription drugs and begin to change her life for the better. Using ECT along with re-discovering Christianity was giving her a whole new outlook on life. She came to know herself on a deeper level and thus was now better equipped to cope with reality in ways that were beneficial rather than self-destructive.

Many clients try to self-medicate, which can take myriad forms. Some like going to the casino and playing the slots, or maybe having a few beers. They are using these things as a way of trying to avoid loss or grief. What they fail to recognize, however, is that these feelings are a natural and normal part of life. When using Emotional Core Therapy to treat depression, clients must learn the proper coping mechanisms for processing grief. The time varies from person to person and from one situation to another. The severity of the situation makes a big difference. Losing a five-dollar bill is not going to cause as much as grief as finding out that you have cancer. The real problem with drowning your pain away or numbing yourself is that it does not work. It only delays the inevitable: at some point you have to fully grieve the loss.

Another major problem is that addictions dull the five senses, which then hampers our ability to identify the four authentic feelings. Take for example someone who has lost his job and then goes out and drinks eight beers a day for a month. This dulls ALL FOUR of the authentic feelings. Not only grief, which is what they intended to dull, but also joy, fear and relief. The whole body, including the muscular and skeletal system, will be adversely impacted. There is less chance of learning to identify authentic feelings, or to learn your body's responses, or how to relax. You can't work towards bringing more joy into your life, because you are numb. You also cannot effectively process feelings of grief. Day in and day out I hear of people, especially the young, who are told, "Take this drug or that drink and your pain will go away."

ECT demonstrates the fallacy of this poor advice. The truth is, you are sabotaging your chance of recovering.

Emotional Core Therapy teaches us to calm the body by staying in a peaceful, meditative state throughout the day. By remaining this way for a prolonged period you can identify all fearful and toxic events in your life. This includes drugs or alcohol. A person that understands how a hot stove works would not touch it because they understand that it causes burns and pain. The same can be said for drugs and alcohol. Why would you use something that could cause legal and financial trouble? Why would you use something that could cause sensory deprivation?

None of this is to suggest that the causes of addiction, or treating them, are simple. There are many reasons why people do drugs: some do it for experimentation, others use it as a mild form of relaxation and there are many other reasons beyond those. With alcohol, a small amount can even be good for you, as can a glass of lemon tea. Yet there is a dramatic difference between four glasses of wine and four glasses of lemon tea! The wine drastically dulls your ability to experience the four authentic feelings. This is doubly destructive, because the more one dulls the senses, the less success ECT can achieve.

A relationship with drugs or any addiction can be very dangerous and can cause long-term damage to your system, especially highly addictive drugs such as cocaine. How to alleviate the dangers? The more information one has about illicit drugs or alcohol, the less likely they will be to use them. Would someone really want to use methamphetamine (also known as "speed"), for example, if they knew the harm that it could cause to their body, or heroin, if they fully understood that an overdose could kill them? As if that weren't bad enough, with illegal drugs nobody knows exactly what is in it, meaning it often includes toxic substances that can be deadly. You need to notify your medical doctor when you have any mental health problems, but especially problems with addictions, because medical doctors have a good understanding of these issues (especially when harmful chemicals are involved) and how to address them. Over the years I have worked with a variety of addictions. This includes addictions to prescription drugs, cigarettes, alcohol, marijuana, narcotics, pornography, and junk food. ECT is a very helpful approach to addictions because it forces the client to examine all the relationships they are choosing to enter in their lives. When a client sees they are bringing fear and grief into their lives by acquiring an addiction they are more responsive to changing their behaviors. Why bring pain and suffering to your body along with possible legal and financial trouble? Why not work towards relationships that can bring you joy? An important point in treating addictions is to be kind and compassionate to the client suffering addiction. Anger pulls people away from communicating. When a therapist can bring up the dangers of a toxic relationship (such as most addictions) in a calm manner, the client is more receptive to learning. Oftentimes people need to get valuable information about addictions to make informed changes. It is very empowering for clients to make their own healthy decisions away from an addictive lifestyle. I often tell my clients that a healthy and supportive relationship with friends or family that can bring you joy is a great way to live. We will cover the topic of addictions in detail later in the book.

Getting back specifically to ECT's treatment of depression, it can be very creative in the ways that it supports patients. For example, one woman I talked to remembered the classic song by The Fifth Dimension called, "One Less Bell to Answer." It's about a woman whose husband has died and she is emotionally devastated, in her despair agonizing over why did he have to leave me? We talked about that song, and sometimes we even play songs in therapy as a tool. There is something soothing not only in the singer's heart-rending voice and words, but also in the song's rhythmic chorus and hauntingly smooth music. It helps relieve some of the grief to talk about whatever it is that hurts us, and it's a great way to help release feelings.

One of the reasons that music is such an excellent technique to release feelings is the sheer magnitude of songs. Some artist has recorded a song for nearly every possible type of relationship issue or problem. All four authentic feelings have hundreds, if not thousands of songs that people can relate to in every culture and virtually every personal situation. For example, consider the song, "All My Sorrows, Sad Tomorrows," by the group, The Marmalade. Its lyrics allow one to daydream and reflect on their own sorrowful past in a calm but sad manner.

Another tool might be to talk about movies, maybe a medical one. For instance, a client talked about a movie in which a man had to endure his young son's terrible illness, trying to find a cure for most of the movie. This drama was called "Lorenzo's Oil," and it was such a sad movie that it would bring tears to the viewers' eyes with the tragic sequence of events that unfold for the little boy. Another movie, "Ladder 49," was about a man dying in a fire. He was a very well-liked fireman who was devoted to putting out fires. In this movie the rest of the firefighters, as well as the man's family and community, are devastated by the loss of his life. When a viewer watches this type of film it is possible to evoke some hidden feelings of loss. This kind of reading of toxic feelings happens to most of us daily in some fashion when we maybe watch a soap opera or perhaps listen to a sad song on the car radio. None of this is meant to be morbid. The point is, hiding from grief does not make it go away and it does not cure depression. To the contrary, identifying the feelings of loss, is the first step in coping with those feelings, and sometimes things like songs and movies can help us put our finger on the problem spot.

The one common factor in all of the examples we are discussing is that they are all about loss. But simply knowing that is not enough. We need to explore deeper, to get to the roots of what these relationships were truly about.

Another client, Tony, was dealing with a different set of circumstances. He did not have a great voice in his family, and consequently never really had anyone to confide in. His father was a hard driving workaholic, so Tony worked hard too. He took a job position out of state, spent a lot of night hours at work, and didn't have many friends (and the few he did have worked regular day hours). Worse yet for Tony, he lived in a secluded subdivision that did not have many young people living nearby. So his issue coming to therapy was isolation and despair, which are terms otherwise known as loss or grief.

Using the authentic nature of ECT, I was able to show Tony how his feelings of grief were connected to his lack of friends and support. In therapy, I was able to draw a small picture of how the four authentic feelings work and Tony was able to see that his pervasive feelings of sadness were situational to his job, relocating out of state, and moving away from friends. When Tony began counseling with my office he was near a nine on the one to ten-point scale of sadness ratings. This was however a temporary state. We discussed Tony's childhood where he was often very happy playing ice hockey with friends back in his hometown. He was able to see his feelings of grief were tied to entering a new relationship (new job in new town)

As part of our therapy, Tony made a list of ten things that would bring him joy. His top five wishes were a new house, new car, a vacation in Hawaii, a new girlfriend, and new friends.

Over the course of the next 14 months, Tony began to work towards those five dreams that would bring him joy. He was able to achieve two to three of his desired ways to bring joy into his life. His level of grief plummeted from an eight or nine to two to four as Tony began to feel more supported and loved in his life.

In therapy, he was honest about his feelings. He genuinely wanted to get better. One of the first big decisions he made was to move closer the where there were more people. In his new home nearer to town he could walk around, go to shops, and be near people. This made him feel more connected not only to the community, but to life itself. You see, it was important for Tony to build a support network so that he would not feel so isolated.

A big part of that support network snapped into place when Tony joined the local church. He had grown up believing in Jesus, but as a teenager became less interested in his religion. It simply didn't seem very important to him. He was just too preoccupied with so many other things in his everyday life.

But now, as he attended services every week, he started to realize how studying the Word of God could truly change his life. Almost every sermon included a reminder to "be in the word," and he found that to be good advice. As Tony read the Bible, time after time he would learn valuable lessons and insights from it.

After reading the Scriptures, especially some of the Psalms that emphasized God's loving presence, Tony always felt less alone. He felt as though the Lord were speaking to him directly and as a result he began to experience the tranquility that had been missing from his life.

He also came to a deeper understanding of what the Bible means when it speaks of the Body of Christ. He started looking upon his fellow church-goers as his brothers and sisters. A true extended family, something that he needed at this point in his life more than ever before.

And as Tony used the principles that he was learning through ECT, it seemed to buttress the various lessons that he would acquire through the minister's sermons each week and through his own personal Bible reading. ECT affirmed Tony's sense of self-esteem and of focusing his mind in healthy ways. One day he was reading the Epistle to the Philippians (in the New Testament) and the Apostle Paul said: "whatever things are true, whatever things are noble, whatever things are just, whatever things are pure, whatever things are lovely, whatever things are of good report; if there is any virtue and if there is anything that is praiseworthy—meditate on these things."

Wow! These words sounded very much like what he was learning through ECT, and Tony felt sure that, although he still had a long way to go, he now was at least on the right path.

Emotional Core Therapy uses various techniques to help people help themselves to get better. In this case, Tony needed to know that he was worthy to be loved. We helped him to recognize what he wanted out of life. He wanted a girlfriend, a house, a new car, a vacation and a family of his own. At the time, he had none of these things, but he recognized that he could work for them and – most critically – he had the power to get them.

The ECT therapist is like a cheerleader: very supportive of the patient. They go at their own speed and of their own volition. It wasn't the therapist's role to tell Tony what to do. He, like every patient, has to work that out on his own. The therapist is there to support him, trying different things, to assist him in his journey to recovery. In Tony's case, he went online and found a partner after joining a Christian dating service. He started to feel much better. It helped when he started volunteering, which led to him feeling a better quality of life and happier.

The therapist helps the patient to not be fearful about obtaining what they want from life. In ECT, we talk about basic feelings so if there is something that you are afraid of, we want to explore that. We teach people to be respectful of themselves and to acknowledge that they are indeed worthy of working everything out. No, it doesn't come overnight. For example, in Tony's situation he was able to achieve two of his goals, but not all of them – at least not initially. But what really matters is that he was able to bring joy into his life. That was missing when all of his focus was on his depression and he felt utterly powerless to do anything about it.

A third client named Julie was a woman who worked as a Claims Processor. She loved her work. Or, more accurately, she loved spending time with friends at work. The time that she spent on breaks, lunch, etc., were at the center of her social life. That was when she would talk with her friends about anything and everything, and she truly relished those special moments.

But then something quite unexpected happened. The company closed down and all of the employees – i.e., Julie and all of her friends – had to look for other jobs. For her it was devastating, like the loss of a partner or a child. She really cared about these people, and losing them caused her tremendous grief. We worked on ECT therapy for two or three months on how to process that grief. Julie's husband didn't have the training to help her with this, and she realized that she needed outside assistance. ECT allowed her to tell the stories of her pain and to process her feelings in ways that were healthy and promoted mental healing. Julie began to identify and label her authentic feelings of grief in therapy. Early on sessions were filled with crying and feeling angry with her company for sending everyone termination notices. Julie spent hours talking about how much fun she had with her coworkers on her coffee breaks and at lunch. As I explained to Julie, there is no magic cure or pill for grief. It is a necessary part of life. We can only learn from the pain and become better individuals in the future. In Julie's case, she decided that she needed more female companions outside of work. She did not want to experience this devastating loss ever again in her life.

Using and processing authentic feelings of joy and grief in therapy, Julie recognized that she needed to build her female support network outside of work. One way in which she did this was to become more involved with her local church. A Baptist from childhood, Julie had gotten into the habit of pretty much only attending services on holidays or other special occasions. But she then joined a group of volunteers (mostly women) who served the homeless at a church sponsored soup kitchen. The sense of camaraderie amongst women who shared her faith and her commitment to helping others brought a good deal of happiness into her life. Amongst other things, it helped her to realize that people experience all kinds of hardships in this world, but the companionship of good friends or even the kindness of complete strangers can help to turn things around.

The lessons that she was learning in Bible study were also crucial to her improving mental outlook. She especially focused on stories of redemption where God rewarded believers for their faith and never giving up when it came to hoping in Him for their salvation. Her outlook improved whenever she meditated on these promises from the Lord.

She was able to learn from her debilitating feelings of sadness and have more hope for the future. Just as our aspiring gymnast in an earlier example was better off learning from her painful ankle injury, Julie was in turn better off for processing and identifying her four authentic feelings of joy, grief, fear, and relief. She was able to recognize that the foreign feelings her body was manifesting as symptoms (fatigue, lack of sleep, trouble concentrating) were signs that her relationship with work was out of balance. Julie's central nervous system was reacting negatively to the relationship (job termination) that she was experiencing leaving. She was determined to make better decisions about when and where to make friends.

Oftentimes clients like Julie need a hug, tissue, and a non-judgmental atmosphere to release their foreign feelings of sadness. To Julie's credit she was a visual learner. We were able to diagram her supportive relationships and identify and isolate her feelings of loss. Both the visual and verbal means of expression allowed Julie to cathartically release her sadness over a period of a few months. The goal was to help her work towards making new friends, both in and out of work so that she could strike the proper balance in her life.

Julie began to garden to regain her sense of calm and peace. By gardening, Julie was able to begin her process of self-care and self-soothing. Early in this book we mentioned how gardening can be a way to relax and meditate. For Julie this worked like a charm. It is important to again reiterate that what works for one client as a form of relaxation may not work for another. Julie's mind was allowed to daydream and relax when she gardened. Other people may find gardening a chore and mentally taxing. It is an important step in Emotional Core Therapy to find a way to allow the mind a way to daydream and flow freely.

For Julie, ECT reinforced many of the things that she was learning from her renewed interest in her faith. The minister at her church spoke often of having a "personal relationship with Jesus Christ." Julie loved this concept, because as she came to feel closer to Jesus, she felt less alone. He was always there for her and oftentimes she would speak to Him not only in her mind, but out loud in actual spoken words. Processing her emotions became much easier when she could share with the Lord everything that was in her heart and on her mind. She could share all of her fears and anxieties with Him, which felt like an enormous burden lifted off of her shoulders. Practicing ECT can teach you how to have a peaceful, loving relationship with your God throughout the day. What religious person does not want that?

One other case that demonstrates ECT's effectiveness in treating depression involved a construction worker named Gary, a twenty-seven-year old man who had a girlfriend that he loved and adored. He worked for the family business, and the idea had been that he was supposed to make a lot of money following in his father's footsteps. But his father whom he worked for was very demanding. Moreover, the young man worked outside in the cold a lot, which he didn't really like at all.

In ECT therapy, we let him talk out his feelings. He shared things about himself, such as that when he was in high school he was a very good athlete. He was able to recognize and identify the things in life that brought him joy. These included working closely with people; he actually preferred to be working inside, not outside. As a matter of fact, he found great satisfaction working with customers.

Gary could not shake his depression until he changed several of his relationships which were causing him grief. He was sad that he had to work underneath a demanding and mean spirited father. Gary was also sad that he had to work in an isolated job as a construction worker which meant he had to work more outside in cold weather with objects versus working with people inside in a warm office.

When Gary came to see me his level of sadness/depression was at an eight or nine! Fortunately for Gary, he had the time and determination to alter his relationships that were causing him grief. Over the course of twelve months, he was able to quit his job and go back to school to be retrained. Gary came back to visit me a year after therapy ended to report that he had proudly earned employee of the month at his new, much happier job. His level of depression dropped from a nine to a one or two in just over a year.

Let's now try and examine Gary's case of depression through the eight step ECT Flowchart. The first step of the ECT Flowchart is realizing that entering and leaving relationships is what causes one stress. Relationship stress can occur with the relationship we have with ourselves, other people, places, or things. For Gary, step one was recognizing that he entered into some new relationships with his father at work in the construction industry which were causing him stress.

Step two of the ECT process is understanding that each relationship we enter into has various needs that have to be met. These needs are what cause stress. The four categories of needs are emotional, financial, spiritual, and physical. Some relationships require only one or two of the four needs. Others may require all four needs. In Gary's case, the needs of the job were excessive for him. He was required to work long hours (physical) outside in the cold. He was yelled at (emotional) often by his father who didn't pay him very well (financial).

Step three of the Eight Step Flowchart is understanding how our senses perceive stressful needs. Our five senses are hearing, touching, smelling, tasting, and seeing. This step happens quite automatically for most people, including Gary. Gary recognized his stress through hearing his dad yelling at him, touching the cold, and seeing his finances dwindle over time.

Step four of the Eight Step Flowchart is examining which authentic feeling (joy, grief, fear, or relief) arises with the new relationship you have entered. In the case of Gary, he had immense grief from his working relationship with his dad's company. Although there were many aspects of the work relationship that caused him grief, the cold weather, lack of pay, and anger he felt from his dad, were all primary sources.

Step five of the ECT Flowchart is when these emotions get sent to our brain, which is part of the central nervous system. The central nervous system sends messages to our muscular and skeletal system. This step happens automatically for almost all people, including Gary.

Step six is understanding how these uncomfortable symptoms affect our body in the form of muscle tension and tightness, etc. Gary recognized the sinking feeling in his chest, the loss of hope, and crying spells as signs of stress.

Step seven of the ECT process is the releasing process. Learning to discharge toxic emotions. In Gary's case we used many types of techniques to release emotions. One that was very effective was daily journaling, where he wrote down exactly what he felt.

Step eight of the ECT process is balancing your equilibrium and practicing your daily meditative exercises. For Gary, praying to God or other spiritually-centered exercises would not have been appropriate. He was a secular minded person who did not have any strong religious affiliations or religious beliefs. His concentration was more on the here and now details of everyday life. It is important for Christians and indeed people of all faith traditions, to realize that a secular perspective such as Gary's is completely compatible with ECT, too, and it works just as well as religious approaches do for people who are devout. In Gary's case, he used daily swimming at the health club as a time to regroup and calm himself down. When Gary swam, he was able to get his stress out of his body and feel warm and relaxed.

As I mentioned earlier in the book, the ECT process and Flowchart can be used successfully to identify and process nearly any future stress you encounter in life. There has rarely been a human encounter that I can't comprehend using ECT. On rare occasions, the external relationships we enter into are multiple in a short period of time so it is hard to distinguish exactly which needs caused you stress. For example, jogging on a hot, humid day and stopping off for a burrito. When eating your burrito, you put extra hot sauce on it and down a liter of Pepsi. Afterwards you feel terrible and have excess grief. It may not be possible to pin down exactly what caused your stomach to be upset and for you to feel grief. The important aspect to remember is that your true feeling is grief so you won't be repeating that behavior anytime soon.

Once you learn ECT you will have the confidence needed to pick healthy relationships in your life. It takes repetition and practice but the benefits far outweigh the effort needed to learn ECT. As you read the cases presented throughout the rest of the book, keep the ECT process in your mind. Try and visualize each step that the characters in the book are engaging in in their stressful scenarios. ECT can also be used to examine any routine stress such as throwing out your back lifting a heavy object or missing a free throw in basketball. As a reminder, ECT is the only psychological approach, religious teaching, or educational approach that can successfully release the root cause of relationship stress without redirecting your emotions away from how you truly feel. Our four true emotions help us navigate our way through life. The more we can learn about these four emotions. The easier time we will have choosing healthy relationships that make us happy. With ECT, we now have a process that can successfully treat the situational stress that weakens human beings from time to time. ECT can treat this stress effectively because it addresses the root cause of the problem which is the arousal of one of the four true feelings.

Of course, no two people experience depression in the exact same way or for the exact same reasons. Therefore, we always need to treat people as individuals with unique problems and solutions that depend upon their own particular circumstances. However, Emotional Core Therapy offers solutions based on abilities that all of us innately possess. The therapy is successful because it works with your emotions rather than treating them as some kind of enemy or outsider. Depression and sadness, after all, are natural aspects of life, but the sooner and more precisely we understand what brings them about, the closer we are to moving on to a happier and more peaceful frame of mind.

ECT Flow Chart

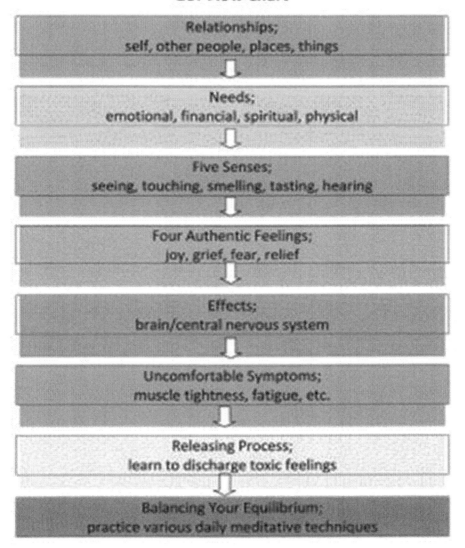

Relationships;
self, other people, places, things

⬇

Needs;
emotional, financial, spiritual, physical

⬇

Five Senses;
seeing, touching, smelling, tasting, hearing

⬇

Four Authentic Feelings;
joy, grief, fear, relief

⬇

Effects;
brain/central nervous system

⬇

Uncomfortable Symptoms;
muscle tightness, fatigue, etc.

⬇

Releasing Process;
learn to discharge toxic feelings

⬇

Balancing Your Equilibrium;
practice various daily meditative techniques

List Five Relationships That You Have Exited That Have Brought You "Grief"

A) MOVING OUT OF STATE

B) FAILING A CLASS AT SCHOOL

1)

2)

3)

4)

5)

NOTES:

List Five Ways You Can Release Feelings Of Grief

A) JOURNALING

B) SINGING

1)

2)

3)

4)

5)

Symptoms Of Depression

Crying spells for no apparent reason

Loss of interest or pleasure in normal activities

Changes in appetite

Fatigue, tiredness and loss of energy

Feelings of sadness or unhappiness

Irritability or frustration, even over small matters

Indecisiveness, distractibility and decreased concentration

List Five Of Your Own Symptoms Of Depression

1)

2)

3)

4)

5)

NOTES:

CHAPTER THREE
Using ECT to Treat Anxiety

As we begin the chapter on anxiety, my hope is that one is beginning to get a basic grasp of the fundamentals of Emotional Core Therapy. As we learn about the use of ECT in a variety of life situations throughout the remainder of this book, my goal is for you to grasp the ECT concepts with as little fear as possible.

Remember, to truly learn anything of value, two things must occur. First, the concept – in this case ECT – needs to be stored in your long-term memory. Second, the concept needs to be practiced or utilized on a frequent basis. As I mentioned briefly in Chapter One, information has to be stored in one's short-term memory until finally it is committed to long-term memory. How many times one needs to practice the concept of ECT varies from person to person. Hopefully, the various situations that we examine taking place in this book seem familiar and realistic, which will help you begin to feel comfortable with the process. My belief is that people can learn ECT when comfortably relaxed. This is why I examine multiple scenarios of diverse people working through their problems in a straightforward fashion. After several different stories the main idea begins to sink in as you gain an increasing understanding of the key ECT concepts.

One of the most powerful tools that ECT offers is the early identification of toxic feelings. In this chapter you will examine in detail the debilitating feeling of "fear" (otherwise known as anxiety). As we discussed in the beginning of this book, fear is caused by entering a relationship that you dislike. A good example of someone entering a relationship they dislike would be a soldier going off to war. Any normal human being that has to put themselves in the line of gunfire would be fearful or afraid. All of the cases we will examine in this chapter have characters entering relationships that they dislike.

The first example that we use involves a young man in his early twenties named Drew. He came to my office complaining of feeling scared about his life. He was nervous that he was not his usual self. He was terrified that he was not living up to being a man. He joined the military, but once he got to boot camp he had a difficult time fulfilling the rigorous requirements and ultimately dropped out. Drew became worried about his self-esteem, and he felt weak for not being able to successfully complete boot camp. The experience was very demanding on the young recruit. The drill instructor was mean spirited, hostile and angry all day long. Drew would wake up at the crack of dawn with the drill instructor yelling at him. He would then be ordered around all day and night by this very demanding guy. Drew was pushed to his limits both physically and mentally during his thirty-day ordeal that included shooting guns off, sleep-deprivation, hot sun, and severe weather conditions.

When we examine some of the feelings that Drew faced we see that he used words such as terrified, nervous and scared. The primary feeling was fear – especially of failing family and friends. Some of Drew's symptoms included a loss of attention, lack of sleep, lack of concentration and fatigue. These are all classic examples of someone who is suffering from fear and anxiety.

For Drew a full recovery would occur within a few months of the counseling. A supportive environment for him to release his feelings of fear would be paramount to his recovery. The focus of treatment would be releasing Drew's traumatic experience. I emphasize traumatic because each situation is different for each individual. For example, there were young men in Drew's boot camp class who were able to successfully graduate without any psychological stress. Some people perceive situations as more stressful than others. So we have to honor each person's fear and how it impacts them.

Part of Drew's success in counseling was that he was able to fully express all the harmful events that happened to him. Moreover, because of his time in the counseling office, he learned that it was okay to express what was on his mind. In fact, it was very important to his recovery. With Emotional Core Therapy, an accepting and non-judgmental ambience is essential in order to trust the process. Even the most horrendous thoughts or feelings are allowed to be expressed, whether they are accurate or not. We sort those out. I gave Drew several examples to practice releasing feelings at home. He was able to choose from a variety of ways to release his feelings. That's what we do with all of our clients. We give them the option to choose what they want to do based on their own world experience and what they like to do.

Some of the ideas include writing, journaling, drawing, listening to music, exercising, jogging, meditation, yoga, or Pilates to name a few. Drew began to feel comfortable in therapy because he chose to freely verbalize his feelings. He started to do more talking, too, which he wasn't used to doing at home, where his family didn't really support expressing his feelings. Once he got into therapy, Drew became more expressive and he started to like it.

Drew was raised as a Christian, and although as an adult he did not consider himself to be an extremely religious man, he did believe in God and he was always fascinated by Jesus. He attended church a few times a year for the most important of the religious holidays such as Christmas and Easter and contributed whenever he could to charities. The words of Jesus about helping one's neighbor always resonated with Drew, and it made him feel good to do his own small part.

As Drew learned more about ECT, and the necessity of verbalizing his feelings, he decided that in addition to his counselor he should speak with the pastor at his local church as well. Pastor Andrews was a very wise man whose mere presence started making Drew feel better and not so alone with his dilemma.

One valuable piece of advice that the pastor offered was for Drew to read the Bible and concentrate on the various characters it portrayed and the harsh adversities that they had faced both as individuals and collectively for the church. For example, Pastor Andrews had him read about the life of the Apostle Paul as depicted in the Book of Acts. Though he survived a shipwreck, was severely beaten in several cities where he preached and then thrown out, was bitten by a venomous snake and ultimately tossed into a dungeon, he nonetheless persevered. He became the most prolific of the New Testament writers and made a profound influence on the world. Though Drew had already been somewhat familiar with Paul's story, he felt as though he was now reading it with fresh eyes.

Drew came to understand that the only way to ever establish any true and lasting peace in his life was for him to learn to love and respect himself as being made in the image of God. In fact, that is one of the essential teachings of Christianity, which describes Christ as the "second Adam". So Drew took great comfort in realizing that making mistakes and sometimes failing is simply part of being human (after all, Adam ate the forbidden fruit!). But through Jesus Christ, God has given humanity a second chance by offering us His steadfast love, mercy and forgiveness. Moreover, through ECT Drew was learning how to love and forgive himself.

Now, none of this meant that Drew was expecting some kind of direct divine intervention, i.e., a miracle. However, it really did help his peace of mind knowing that God is always there for him, and will help him though the storms and trials of life just as Jesus calmed the raging sea that had terrified His followers in that famous Gospel story.

Every client is different in how they choose to express themselves. The best way for a therapist to do ECT is to work from a client's perspective and worldview. For Drew, learning to verbalize his unwanted feelings was a huge emotional growth step. He realized over time that it was okay to talk about negative feelings and to show his vulnerabilities. Drew also began to realize the value of cathartically releasing his feelings. He learned how to self-monitor his body for changes in his physical state, and realized that he was getting better as he started to release his feelings. Consequently, his fear level went down.

To examine how ECT helped Drew recover in this situation let's go back to the diagram in Chapter One on authentic feelings. Our brain receives authentic feelings such as fear. Once our brain, which is part of our central nervous system, senses these feelings, the muscles in our body respond. This sequence of events is helpful for our survival as human beings. If one is having trouble understanding this concept think of a situation which has occurred to most of us at home, touching at hot stove. If you accidentally touch a hot stove and burn your finger, you are not likely to repeat this mistake again. Why? We sense the fear as a result of the negative consequence that the action has on our body, i.e., a burnt finger and the accompanying pain. As for Drew, in therapy he learned to monitor his body and to pay attention to his body's feelings. The symptoms that he experienced were not normal so we try to pay attention to those and over time monitor their slowly dissipating.

Another step in Drew's recovery was the use of meditation and relaxation in his life on a daily basis. Drew had nightmares for months prior to entering therapy so it was important for him to learn to have a quiet state of being as part of his daily life. Every person in therapy relaxes in a different way. One person may like sitting in a Jacuzzi, while someone else might like yoga or Pilates, and others might like to do relaxing activities like bowling or walking a dog. The key to relaxing is to have the mind be free of tension, to be able to daydream, to reflect and be able to stay calm. The key is to have a low level of cognition. Cognition is where you are actually thinking and using your mind actively. We don't want that; we want the mind to freely flow and to reflect. This differs for each person because each person relaxes in a different way. Another term for relaxation is self-soothing. Everybody self-soothes in different ways so we have to go to their point of view. When we talk about different techniques of relaxation, what's good for one person is not necessarily good for another. Let's take sewing for example. One person may find sewing relaxing and they can release feelings that way. But another person may find sewing very stressful because it's physically taxing or they may not know how to do it.

So you have to really pay attention to what each person feels helps his or her mind to relax. We have to go back to their history of what they did when they were younger to relax, and we always give people the option of what they want to do to relax. When we examined Drew's history we found that he enjoyed sitting in his room listening to music. While listening to different artist express themselves and their feelings Drew slowly felt his tensions easing away. This process, however, takes time. Once Drew was able to see how authentic feelings operate, he began to release his feelings. His recovery started when he realized that he didn't have to enter boot camp anymore. That was a situation and a relationship that he had entered into but it was separate from himself and he realized that he would never have to go back to it again. That was an important step for him and a critical component of Emotional Core Therapy, realizing that all relationships either grow or die. He realized that his relationship with boot camp was in the past, that he was separate from that and he could now start to release that fear. By doing this, Drew was finally able to take back control over his life. Once he understood that he was over this experience he could start to release the pain of it.

All the experiences that Drew had gone through in boot camp were separate from himself. He entered into these relationships and he left them. In therapy, he was reminded that he succeeded in other events, so why not this event?

Another key for Drew was releasing pain through nature. Things such as trees and water, open land and spaces help the mind to daydream and wander. With ECT, a client like Drew does not have to be alone, he has an expert therapist side by side helping him sort out his traumatic feelings. Almost certainly Drew would be overwhelmed at the onset of therapy. On a daily basis the sorting out and releasing of his debilitating feelings of fear and loss would help to calm him down and get him back to a balanced equilibrium.

One question we need to ask is why would Drew not be able to release his feelings? With ECT we recognize that the body has a way of protecting itself from foreign or outside feelings. It is not normal and healthy to have debilitating feelings of fear and loss in our lives. If you don't believe what I'm saying, envision a two-year-old girl or boy in a crib. If a two-year-old child has suffered the psychological pain of being yelled at or scolded constantly what would happen? By the same token what would happen if this two-year-old was in his yard and a strange dog came up barking in his face? Quite naturally, the child would start crying to show fear. The child would show visible pain and look for comfort. What would be the remedy? Quite possibly it would be a loving hug from a mommy or daddy or to take the boy away from the dog or the yard where the fearful event had occurred. If bitten, maybe a Band-Aid to stop the bleeding or a visit to the doctor for a shot to make sure that there are no diseases of infections. Every normal and healthy parent would do all that they could to help the child in pain. Why? Because a child cannot do these things themselves, and a two-year-old child cannot lie and deceive themselves about how they feel. They cannot hide pain. They have to release it somehow.

It is a natural process to release emotional pain by crying and whining. They have no defense mechanisms to block the cognitive emotions. Every loving parent would do whatever they could to protect this two-year-old and quite naturally console their pain. Why? The parent loves the child. It is a very powerful relationship. This same power of love is what has to transpire for Drew to get better. He has to respect himself enough to cheer himself and allow himself to get better. It was not a short process for full recovery but so long as Drew had the support of people around him a full recovery was expected. You see, the human body has a natural way of protecting us from danger. The psychological angst of sustaining things like fear and loss is dangerous to the human body. Drew has to allow himself to be held, comforted, and supported to be protected, just like this two-year-old. He has to respect himself and his feelings enough to allow himself to heal from this pain.

We are now ready to examine some other cases where ECT has helped clients to overcome debilitating fear and anxiety. One case involves a successful mortgage specialist who owned a small company. William was divorced for a long time before he met his new wife, Kathy. Together they decided to start a family. Kathy already had one boy prior to meeting William. William had been quite happy with his life the previous ten years before he met Kathy and liked who he was as a person. When he came to my office in a panic, he was in a minor meltdown. He didn't know what the problem was with himself, and he felt like he was falling apart. He couldn't sleep, he couldn't concentrate, had trouble eating and he couldn't feel comfortable around people anymore. He couldn't even be intimate with his wife because he was so stressed out. His level of fear on a scale of one to ten was a nine or ten, in other words, intolerable. So I recommended like I do to all my clients to see a medical doctor when they enter therapy and the doctor can decide whether or not medical treatment is needed. With any counseling whether it's ECT or some other form of therapy, you want to make sure their doctor is notified if they desire it. Some will say they do not want to do so, while others will say that's fine. In William's case, he did not want to take medication even though he was having trouble sleeping. But it was important to get his sleeping in order so that he could start to recuperate because sleep is a recuperative process that you need to reinvigorate yourself. So for a short time William was on medication so that he could sleep better and calm himself down. He was adamant, however, that he didn't want to be on medication long term.

William was a very intelligent man who was able to identify his authentic feelings pretty quickly in his first couple of months of therapy, along with the real cause of his stress. After a brief examination of his life he saw that he was in control of most of his life. He was happy with his job, with his life, and with his support group of friends. He had a sixteen-year-old stepson name Steve. The stepson frequently yelled at William and disrespected him. He called William names, he came home late, disobeyed rules at home, smoked pot, and was taking money from the house. He refused to follow rules. This unruly boy would come and go as he wanted, breaking curfew, getting into legal trouble, and not doing his homework. For William, who was always taught to be kind and respectful, this was his first experience raising a boy. Over the course of several months of ECT, William was able to recognize that he suffered from excessive fear. He started to outline where his fear was coming from. He had fear of being a poor husband to his loving wife, fear of being a poor father, losing control of his life, and fear that he was losing control of his mind and body.

It was clear to William that he did not agree with or condone this boy's behavior. William began to identify the root causes of his debilitating fear. He had chosen to enter into a relationship that caused him fear. In therapy, we worked on how to release that fear. We identified and made a list of all of the things that were causing him fear and slowly worked on reducing fear on each one. We also worked on different techniques for reducing stress. One of them was William's love of jogging, which is an excellent for this purpose. When William was running, he felt that he was more in control of his life. Running also helps to oxygenate the blood and improve the circulatory system, as well as the digestive system. It was also a tension reliever for his muscles. Slowly over time, he was able to work on that as a means of stress relaxation.

This wouldn't be ideal for everyone but it worked well for William. Why? Because when he jogged his mind was able to daydream and release some of these feelings and sort them out. Yet he still wasn't quite happy and balanced. Things do not always work out as planned. Take for example a young couple in their twenties who have a child. Instead of being born healthy this child was born with a birth defect or heart defect. The first few years of the couple's relationship is spent at doctor's offices, not sleeping and excessive financial pain. This could be any situation. The point is things change as you go forward. In William's case he sought relief from excessive fear. By utilizing some of the ECT techniques used by all therapists to relieve stress, William had success distancing himself in the same way that Drew had in boot camp.

The difference between William's case and Drew's was that Drew never had to go back to his relationship with stress. Boot camp was over and done. So Drew was able to leave therapy pretty whole. With William, his stepson was still belligerent and didn't want to go to therapy. So as we examine William's situation it was clear that the boy had displayed power over his stepfather from time to time. William felt helpless. For a brief time, William tried to work on parenting skills with his wife and it helped a little bit. William recognized that he had limited power in this situation and he needed to work on his own situation separate from his stepson. What he did to resolve the situation was to spend less time with his stepson.

It was basically rolling the dice. What he was able to do was to peaceably co-exist with his stepson for about a year and a half. Yet he still suffered debilitating stress. When he started therapy his stress was about a nine or ten, but as he worked some of these ways to relax himself such as jogging and releasing his feelings, by talking in therapy it dropped down to about a five or a six. He didn't get completely better until the boy went off to college. Even then William continued with therapy, and he started to become calmer. He tried different techniques to relieve stress. For instance, he was doing more writing, listening to music, and he got a dog and started walking it throughout the neighborhood. Eventually, he was able to lower his stress to a one or two.

One of the keys for William was to use his strong religious faith to help him lower his stress level. William had been brought up in the Greek Orthodox Church, and he firmly believed in all of its tenets. Attending church services always helped to calm him down and reorient his frame of mind in a more tranquil way. As he would listen to the music and the words of the liturgy as recited by the priest, it went a long way toward sending his thoughts into a peaceful, meditative direction that helped drive out so much of the mental turmoil that lay behind his stress.

William also became more interested in the sacred Orthodox tradition of venerating icons, small sacred images that depict scenes from the life of Christ or of the saints. The idea is to aid and encourage people in strengthening their faith and worship.

When portraying historical scenes, the faces on the icons don't show emotions but instead portray virtues such as purity, patience in suffering, forgiveness, compassion and love. An example of this would be the portrayal of Christ on the cross. Neither is the icon a sentimental picture. Christ is always shown as God. Even the icons of Christ seated on His mother's lap show Him with an adult face, revealing that even though Christ lived as a child among us He was also God.

All of this profound spiritual knowledge, conveyed to William through simple reflection and focusing on an icon during meditation, helped him to feel less stress in his life, regardless of whatever circumstances he may have been facing at the moment.

For Christians of other denominations, the same results could be achieved by different means. One example might be quietly praying in bed and reflecting on a peaceful instance in your life where you strongly felt the presence of Jesus and His blessings. Or it could be similar feelings of tranquility evoked in a group prayer of thanks after a Bible study. What all of these practices have in common is the peace and solace that comes to one's heart and mind when they abandon all of the cares and strife in their life, at least for the moment, and only reflect upon Jesus Christ, His love for us and our devotion to Him.

William continued in therapy for a year or two. He had other situations arise like health issues, and his stress went up again, but because he did ECT he was able to recognize these fears and reduce them too. Later on, he had more and more fears over some of his business clients that were causing him stress, but once again he was able to use ECT and recognize how his body felt. He was able to process his feelings and move forward and become more balanced. This was a person I worked with for five or six years and he was able to do a marvelous job of monitoring his body, identifying fears and having techniques in place to reduce them.

With Emotional Core Therapy, the client has power to enter and leave relationships. William had spent years as an adult not fully understanding his emotions but he never needed professional help before. Now he was able to monitor his body and his authentic feelings and go on with his life. I would call Williams's therapy successful because he was successful in identifying his feelings, recognizing toxic relationships, making choices to reduce stress, getting over relationships and monitoring his body for meditation. He did this to a good degree. That's all we can do with ECT. There is no answer or solution to avoid pain. Therapists cannot make decisions for clients. The client has to make decisions about which relationships that they want to enter into. Sometimes people have been in a toxic situation. You have to be supportive within those situations and try to reduce the stress. The relief may not, however, be instant all the time.

This can be particularly true when dealing with on the job stress. As just about everybody knows, workplace stress can be very demanding on one's psyche. Oftentimes an employer will place demands on their employees that cause excessive fear. For years, the medical community would have their trainees, called residents, work one hundred-hour weeks. Often 14-18 hour days. When the demands on a person are this high, anxiety conditions are likely to develop. This is because anxiety is another word for fear. These medical students had increased fear, or excessive fear related to the tasks of their profession. Fortunately for the medical profession, they began to recognize the issue and make changes. What good is a doctor to his or her children and family if he or she has to be gone all day? Residents were experiencing difficulty, not only with their work, but also with their family relationships. How could they not? Their family members have needs also. We discussed in the Introduction that people have emotional, financial, spiritual, and physical needs. If you are gone out of the house all the time, how can you meet the needs of others?

Workplace stress (or school stress) can vary from person to person depending on many factors. Consider a postman or deliveryman. If the person in this job has an injury or condition with his feet and the job requires walking all day, this job would cause excessive stress. What if another individual has no health problems and enjoys nature, being outside, and helping people. In stark contrast, he may love the job. Two different people, same job, yet different levels of stress. That's because people experience stress differently. Still, if you examine the most stressful jobs in our society, most of them cause excessive fear on a normal human's emotions. Look no further than a soldier, policeman, ironworker, professional football player, or a stay at home mother of five, and you will see a common variable. Most of these jobs require a great deal of tasks to be completed, usually in uncomfortable conditions. Thus, they lead to very high levels of stress.

Emotional Core Therapy is about being human and desiring to stay human. That means honoring and processing the four authentic feelings. If an employer causes excess fear in a person that lasts throughout the day, it becomes a problem. Why? It is difficult to transition from denying your senses at work, to honoring them at home.

Take the case of Lillian, a twenty-nine-year old case adjuster for an insurance company. She came to me, apparently stressed out. She said she couldn't take her job anymore. The job was so stressful that she had trouble sleeping, trouble concentrating, had chest pains, mild tension, classic signs of fear or stress. Her heart was beating fast. She had a fear of being a failure. As we went through therapy, it was clear that her job was very demanding. As an insurance adjuster, from the time she walked in the door until the time she left, her work situation was being monitored. Her supervisor was nearby and could see her in her cubicle. All of her phone calls were being monitored, not just her but everyone in the company for accuracy and professionalism. She had an inbox of responsibilities, and it was always full. She was given a brief break in the morning, a noontime lunch break of 45 minutes and a short break in the afternoon. Lillian was responsible for handling complaints and processing insurance claims. Clients would often yell or scream at her and she was supposed to stay poised and calm at all times. People could be abusive to her and she wasn't able to do anything about it but stay calm. This was a job you could not do forever because it was almost inhuman.

In ECT we were able to compartmentalize Lillian's stress. We examined her statements and the common theme was the acceptance of fear of not being able to meet the demands of her job. In our initial meeting her stress level was a seven or eight out of ten. She knew that she was not the same person that she was used to being for most of her life. As we reviewed her history, we saw that she had been quite calm back in her teens and early twenties and that didn't start to change until she took this job. When we began using ECT, we outlined her thoughts on a piece of paper and enumerated ten different ways that she felt overwhelmed each day. In the first few weeks of therapy we were able to process her feelings and she was allowed to vent them. This provided some momentary relief.

Still, she continued to have a six to eight on her stress level. Over the course of a month, her stress level didn't go down to a one or a two because the root cause of her stress persisted. Her work demands continued to weigh heavily on Lillian; they never changed. Her inbox was still full, and her supervisors were still monitoring her calls. She was even put on probation for a while. Her situation was similar to William's from our second example. William still lived with his disobedient son, which was causing him fear. Both of these situations are relationships that these people entered into and they stayed with them, which is why their level of fear remained high. In a perfect world William would have kicked his stepson out of his house and Lillian would have quit her job and be happy. But in the real world she couldn't do that because she needed the money to pay her mortgage and other expenses.

Both of them were stuck in their current circumstances and they were not going to be able to leave anytime soon. Nonetheless, they were both able to work in the short-term doing some ECT techniques to release their feelings. In Lillian's case, as I often see in therapy, things were okay in other areas of her life such as friends and family even though her work situation was causing her stress. To help reduce her fear, we reviewed some ways that she was able to get peace before taking this job.

Emotional Core Therapy does not promise utopia or a perfect outcome for every client. Indeed, no therapy can offer that. Oftentimes the best one can do is to deal with their life's stresses head on in a more meaningful and manageable way. For Lillian, she was never able to achieve an emotional state of being able to consistently remain calm. Most times in therapy she was a five or a six. That was to be expected, since her demands never changed, and in some cases even got worse. She pursued ECT for a couple of months and it was beneficial to her and allowed her to reframe her mental state. Prior to therapy Lillian would often say to herself, I'm afraid, I'm scared, I'm not doing enough, I'm going to lose my job. No one likes me at work, I'm a failure, something's wrong with me. But ECT allowed this young woman a different mindset. Her frame of thinking now became: I've got a good heart. It's only the job that's causing me excessive fear. I'm able to separate from the job. I recognize that I chose this position and my career here and I'll have to leave this position sometime sooner than I like. But I still realize that I can manage the separation between me and this job.

Through ECT we can learn common techniques to reduce stress. Lillian practiced meditation during her breaks as a way to reclaim herself. Her way of practicing meditation was to pay attention to her calm self. What we tried to do with Lillian was to review what she did before getting the job that helped her to be peaceful. We worked on a calm, steady way to breathe. By taking deep short breaths, she began to slow her thought processes down.

Lillian also told me that her mother used to read to her from the Bible when she was a little girl. Though she had not read the Bible herself much as an adult, Lillian still found great comfort in recalling these stories, and decided to give the Bible some of her time. She came to appreciate the necessity of quieting the mind to foster spiritual growth, and soon realized that these Christian beliefs were highly compatible with ECT. The meditation not only helped to reduce her stress, but it brought her into a deeper realm of spirituality that made her feel better about herself as a child of God and her place in His Kingdom.

As a way to relax, and to increase her newfound understanding of traditional Christian concepts, Lillian focused her Bible reading on the Book of Psalms. She was astonished one day when she came upon the following verse: I will lie down and sleep in peace, for you alone, O LORD, make me dwell in safety. (Psalm 4:8)

These words of wisdom that she now remembered her mom had read to her years earlier before bedtime, fit in perfectly with what she was currently learning from her therapist about ECT. Lillian realized that ECT was designed in such a way that it will help with processing one's emotion regardless of what faith tradition a person adheres to, or none at all. It adapts itself very easily to every individual's thoughts, beliefs and way of living.

Lillian also told me that she had also enjoyed nature when she was young, so we practiced meditating on a beautiful park while she was at work to relax. There was a nature trail near her condo, and she was able to relax by spending time there.

She came to realize that letting go of those feelings of fear and anxiety is important so she also started doing that at work while she was on breaks. In this way she was able to slow her body down. In addition to learning to relax, Lillian would also do some brisk walking to get her mind clear. On her walks she would discover that her heart rate was decreasing and her blood pressure dropping. She learned to monitor her body and started to get calmer.

The key to any successful therapy approach, including ECT is to be honest with one's feelings. Lillian had some basic strengths and she was quite gentle with her life prior to her work assignment. Although Lillian only spent a short time in therapy, she found results with ECT. She began to identify the four authentic feelings and how they affected her, and came to understand the importance of being peaceful and relaxed. She recognized that as an adult, she had the power to enter and leave any relationship or all relationships in her world. In an ideal situation, Lillian would have benefited from six to eight months of doing work with ECT, but she only had a couple of months. That's all she chose to do.

There is a process about Emotional Core Therapy, and like any sound therapy process, one needs to focus time and energy on it to be successful. We can use Lillian as a case study of how it is beneficial as one begins to see ECT as a process. Keep in mind, of course, that ECT can only allow one to regain their humanness. It can never cure cancer, it can't promise eternal happiness, and it can't eliminate all sadness in one's life. No therapy can promise these results. Every new relationship one enters into with people, places and things will cause a response from us as human beings. It will either bring joy or fear. That's simply the way life works. With ECT, however, it can be a happier and more peaceful life, and one that we can live with greater dignity and independence. No one can really predict the future, all we can do is work on releasing feelings and obtaining a meditative state of calmness.

Another case that we can learn from involves a young executive in his thirties named Thomas who ran a successful small business with his father and his mother. Thomas grew up in a close knit family and worked in the family business. He met his wife Betty while in college. They decided to have two kids together, which they did. Betty was very outgoing and loved the nightlife. She gave up her career to raise their kids. When the children were little, Betty decided to restart her music career so she went out at night and sang at nightclubs. She began to experiment with drugs and alcohol and soon engaged in an extramarital affair. Betty had been cheating on Thomas for three months when he came to my office. He didn't know what to do with himself, and he was at his wit's end. He knew that his life with his wife was ending and that their relationship was ending. Thomas wanted to be there for his kids and for his home. He was worried about losing his house and his savings through divorce. This young man had devoted his life to his family and now it was falling apart.

Thomas exhibited several of the classic symptoms of anxiety: he had trouble sleeping, muscle tension, and he lost weight. He had to do a great deal of tasks with his children as his wife was frequently out of the home. With Emotional Core Therapy, Thomas was able to compartmentalize all of his excessive fears. We would write down each fear and discuss the situation in detail. Part of Thomas' excessive fear was financial stress. He was dreading the cost of lawyers, selling the home, the cost of maintenance for his soon-to-be ex-wife, the cost of child support, etc. These were not entirely rational thoughts; they were just excessive fears in case the situation went bad.

Over the course of several months, Thomas was able to come to decisions that helped alleviate his high level of fear. He hired a lawyer and found out that the cost of divorce was not going to be as high as he had feared. Also, during the course of therapy his wife decided not to be the custodial parent, so Thomas didn't have to worry about losing the kids. Betty was okay with Thomas being the primary parent in the home. With ECT we were able to give Thomas perspective on the whole process of ending his marriage. He would still be able to parent but he had to grieve the loss of a partner, which was a grief that he had to identify, but he also had relief from a fearful point of view in that he wasn't going to lose his financial life's savings. When Thomas began to gain symptomatic relief, instead of feeling an eight or nine on a fear scale, he went back down to a five or six in a couple of months and soon afterwards reduced it even further to a three or four.

In the case of Thomas, he had a secular outlook on life. Religious faith had never been very important to him, and although God did not seem to play a major role in his life, it was still important for Thomas and for all secular people to learn how to live a life filled with peace and love, both for himself and towards others. With ECT, Thomas was able to take significant steps in this direction.

After all, when great religions such as Christianity teach to "love thy neighbor as thyself" that is God's call to us to be kind, supportive, and compassionate to others and to ourselves regardless of our particular brand of faith. Or, as with Thomas, if a person has no religion at all.

Regardless of the circumstances, or one's belief, or lack of belief, every single one of us is a child of God deserving of equal love and dignity as every other human soul ever created. The basic human condition, including our needs and even our failings, are the same for all. There are no exceptions to this universal rule.

As therapists we all want what is best for our clients. But we are human just like our clients, and neither the client nor the therapist can predict the future. The end result for Thomas was a positive outcome. However, people need to also learn how to deal with circumstances in life when things don't work out well at all. What if his wife had decided that she had wanted the house or the children? Thomas would still have to work through his fear and loss. He may have needed a therapist for a year and a half instead of just a few months. The point is every situation is different. I was happy to see Thomas get some support and relief in the short-term as he was able to work on his authentic feelings. As we have seen with other situations in this book, sometimes the road to recovery can be longer and harder. Fortunately, Emotional Core Therapy offers a path, a strategy for coping that helps us not only with major crises such as we saw with Thomas, but also with the less drastic (but every bit as real) worries and stressors that all of us contend with in our everyday lives.

Hopefully the "FEAR" you have about comprehending this approach has been alleviated somewhat after reading the anxiety chapter. Feel free to glance at the adjacent flowchart to measure your comprehension of the psychological process we are teaching in this book. Don't worry (otherwise known as fear) if you haven't mastered the entire approach just yet. We will revisit the approach in more detail in the following chapter, "Using ECT to Understand Anger."

ECT Flow Chart

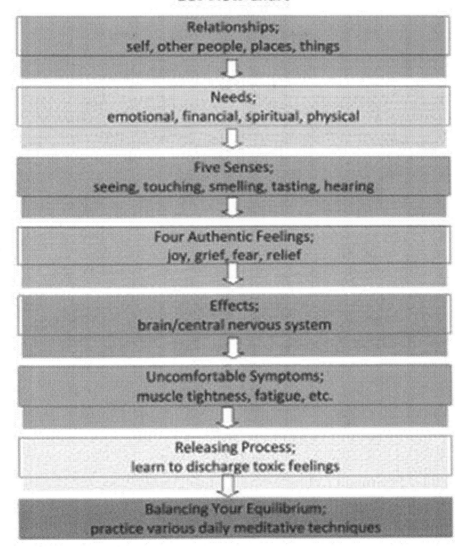

Relationships;
self, other people, places, things

Needs;
emotional, financial, spiritual, physical

Five Senses;
seeing, touching, smelling, tasting, hearing

Four Authentic Feelings;
joy, grief, fear, relief

Effects;
brain/central nervous system

Uncomfortable Symptoms;
muscle tightness, fatigue, etc.

Releasing Process;
learn to discharge toxic feelings

Balancing Your Equilibrium;
practice various daily meditative techniques

List Five Relationships That You Have Entered That Have Caused You Fear

A) PLACING MONEY IN THE STOCK MARKET

B) GOING ON A ROLLER COASTER.

1)

2)

3)

4)

5)

NOTES:

List Five Ways You Can Release Debilitating Feelings Of Fear.

A) Using satire

B) Call a trustworthy friend and chit chat

1)

2)

3)

4)

5)

NOTES:

Symptoms Of Anxiety

Having an increased heart rate

Breathing rapidly (hyperventilation)

Feeling powerless

Having a sense of impending danger, panic or doom

Feeling apprehensive

Sweating

Feeling weak or fatigued

Trembling

List Five Of Your Own Symptoms Of Anxiety

1)

2)

3)

4)

5)

NOTES:

CHAPTER FOUR
Using ECT To Understand Anger

So far, we've mostly been exploring situations where someone has hurt our feelings or harmed us in some way. In this chapter we will examine those circumstances in life where not only someone gets angry at us, but we hurt or harm others with anger. This does not mean that we are bad people. Yet, in our humanness, we see that we all have faults in relationships. There are times when we accidentally or intentionally hurt others in our lives. Examples might be cutting someone off on the highway, speaking out of turn, or skipping to the front of the line at the grocery store when we are in a hurry.

All of us do something like this at least once in a while. The difference, however, between an emotionally healthy person and an abusive person is that the emotionally healthy person truly regrets doing the hurtful or harmful act. Why? They know that hurting someone is destructive in nature. Consider these four very common expressions:

"Treat others as you want to be treated"

"What goes around, comes around"

"Every action has an opposite and equal reaction"

"To err is human, to forgive is Divine"

Each of these aphorisms is intended to make us see things from the other person's point of view. Moreover, Christianity teaches people to promote the virtue of forgiveness and reciprocity in relationships. For example, "Forgive us our trespasses as we forgive those who trespass against us," is a phrase from "The Lord's Prayer". This same sense of fairness and respect for others can be seen using the techniques of Emotional Core Therapy, especially the eighth step, as it releases debilitating feelings of fear and grief. The prayer is cathartic in nature and cleanses the soul.

With ECT we understand that stress (otherwise known as debilitating feelings of fear and grief) is caused by entering and leaving relationships. As we discussed earlier in the book, when we go towards a relationship we like (such as a good friend) there is joy. When we leave something we like (good friend) there is grief. When we go towards something we dislike (heavy traffic during rush hour) there is fear. When we leave something we dislike (there is relief). Since anger is a reaction to grief, what relationship is being stressed? The answer is the relationship you have with yourself. In the cases you will read in this chapter keep in mind that each character who is angry is really grieving his own sense of loss.

We all from time to time have made mistakes that hurt others and brought grief or fear into others' lives. Examples might include yelling at your children or siblings, or "blowing up" at your subordinates at work. The difference is that when you begin to honor your authentic feelings of joy, grief, fear, and relief, you become aware of your uncomfortable muscle and bodily sensations that result from stress. This physical discomfort is a signal that something is wrong with a relationship. With ECT, we recognize that our normal state of being is one of meditation or relaxation. Hence, we become trained to eliminate the debilitating feelings of fear and loss.

Anger is a reaction to grief. People who are angry are in fact, grieving and suffering loss. Each individual varies in their intensity and duration of anger. One of the benefits of using ECT is it helps give us a better grasp of authentic feelings, so we can dig deeper and get to the real roots of someone's anger. We must also realize that anger can affect the central nervous system, so it's important especially as we get older to have less stress on the body, and less anger in one's life. By having less anger and stress, your blood pressure can stay calm and your body can be more regulated.

Let's take an example of an angry woman to see how ECT can help her better her communication skills and in turn get her needs met. The woman in this hypothetical case is named Louise. Louise tells her boyfriend Thomas, "You are such an idiot! You leave the toilet seat up all the time because you are a barbaric slob." Of course, Louise's words are harmful and destructive.

With Emotional Core Therapy, Louise is taught to honor herself as well as others. A better way of stating her grief at being treated poorly in the bathroom might be the following: "Thomas, I am saddened that you have left the toilet seat up again. I feel a sense of loss of respect when my earlier request to keep the bathroom tidy was not heard." It doesn't have to be these exact words, but something that conveys this sentiment in a similar non-accusatory yet frankly honest manner. Such words would stand a better chance of drawing Thomas into the discussion of cleaning the bathroom. In stark contrast, the angry yelling by Louise is likely going to detract from their relationship and push Thomas away from her. The more authentic that Thomas and Louise can be with each other, the closer they will become in their relationship. As people become better at authenticating their four feelings of joy, grief, fear, and relief, they can learn to grow their relationships further and better.

ECT would be likely to help Louise evolve as a human being. It would allow her to use more authentic words such as loss and grief instead of "idiot" and "barbaric slob." These words would help her get more in touch with her inner self. The sooner Louise gets in touch with her core feelings, the sooner she can release them and move on to a healthier state of being. The beauty of ECT is the ability to make the hundreds of feelings simplified into one of the four authentic feelings. By doing so, one has a much better chance of releasing psychic pain and moving on from the negative state of being.

She started becoming more emotionally centered, and when this happens there is less chance to use anger, as it is a reaction to one of the four authentic feelings. As you learn to live in a more authentic way, honoring your feelings, you become less inclined to need anger as a response to relationships. Why would one use anger as a means of communication when there are far better, less destructive options available?

Louise had been a Christian since she was a young child. She gave her heart to Christ at a church revival when she was nine years old. Ever since then, she had learned from her parents and from her church that as Christian believers the focal point of their lives should be establishing and growing a personal relationship with Jesus Christ. True to her beliefs, this relationship was in fact the most important component of Louise's life, and she valued it over and above all other things.

However, as Louise became more knowledgeable about ECT, it made her begin to think about the other relationships in her life, too, most notably with her boyfriend Thomas. Would she ever lash out at Jesus with such anger as she did with Thomas? Of course not! Nonetheless, there were times in her life when she felt angry or upset about her circumstances, and in those situations she would indeed go to Jesus in prayer and spill out all her thoughts and feelings to Him.

The key was honesty, speaking to the Lord from her heart about how she was truly feeling.

Louise came to realize that ECT was asking her to do the same thing with the people in her life, in this case her boyfriend. Express her authentic feelings openly and without ambiguity. When she began speaking to Thomas face to face in much the same way as she opened up her heart to Jesus in prayer, her anger dissipated and as an added bonus before long they were feeling much closer as a couple as well.

Our next example of anger is the hypothetical case of a man named Ted, who is a father of four. He walks into the kitchen one afternoon and sees a pile of dirty dishes. Earlier in the day he had asked his teenaged daughter, Kelly, to wash the dishes. So when he walks into the kitchen later in the day he is shocked to see the dishes still lying in the sink. He loudly yells at Kelly, "What the hell are these dishes still doing here! I told you to do them early this morning. Can't you do what you are told?"

Of course, Ted feels terrible later on about what he did to Kelly. He loves his daughter very much and wonders what is wrong with him that he can't control his anger. Using ECT, we examine the situation for the four authentic feelings. Anger is not one of the four authentic feelings, so what was Ted really feeling? Ted had obviously been shocked when he came into the kitchen and saw the dirty dishes still sitting in the sink. His feeling of grief comes from his perception that the dishes would all be cleaned. In his mind he had envisioned walking into the room and seeing an empty sink with the dishes put away. But what he was really grieving was the loss of feeling respected by his daughter. Ted is simply hurt, but does not know how to process his feelings appropriately.

Let's examine how Ted would approach this situation if he truly had a grasp of Emotional Core Therapy and using the four authentic feelings. He might say, "Hi, Kelly, I know you've been busy but I want to discuss with you how I am feeling. I am a bit sad and hurt that you did not follow through with my request to do the dishes."

Which statement is a better style: 1) "What the hell are these dishes still doing here! I told you to do them early this morning. Can't you do what you are told?" Or, "Hi, Kelly, I know you've been busy but I want to discuss with you how I am feeling. I am bit sad and hurt that you did not follow through with my request to do the dishes." Obviously, the second statement would be better. "Sad" and "hurt" are really just names to describe grief. In the second example where Ted asserts his feelings we have a better chance of drawing Kelly into the conversation.

The feelings of anger that Ted was struggling with were especially difficult for him because, as a practicing Christian, family life was highly important to him. In church, he had heard many sermons about the importance of a strong family as one of the key underpinnings of living a good Christian life. Ted always thought that was one of the most beautiful aspects of the faith and indeed he loved his family very much.

Why then, was he letting his anger come between him and those he loved so dearly, in this case his daughter Kelly?

ECT gave him the answer, his inability to properly release his grief. In therapy he learned several approaches for how to do this, and one suggestion was to embrace his spiritual beliefs more fully when it came to this issue. So Ted began thinking about what the Bible teaches about anger and its consequences. According to the Paul's letter to the Ephesians, holding on to anger gives Satan a pathway into your life: "Do not let the sun go down while you are still angry, and do not give the devil a foothold."

This was great advice! It made Ted realize that every time he let anger come between him and another person, especially a family member, he was giving in to the power of evil and allowing it to run roughshod over his life. This, of course, was the last thing in the world that he would ever want. However, by refocusing his thoughts and words into more positive channels, as he was learning through ECT, Ted would instead be showing his daughter that he loved her, just as Jesus did. Therefore, it was never a good idea to let the day end with unresolved anger eating away at him from the inside out.

Moreover, again as with the Lord, Ted only wanted what was best for his daughter Kelly, and for her to show her love back to him by respecting his authentic feelings. In this way, Ted believed he could better deal with his anger issues and perhaps teach his daughter a valuable spiritual lesson at the same time.

Anger pulls people away from each other and injects fear into the dialogue and it detracts from healthy communication with other human beings. In the long run, Ted will have a much better relationship with Kelly if he can draw her into conversations rather than pull her away by scaring her. Furthermore, in the last chapter we had discussed how fear adversely affects the central nervous system. That is one of the multitude of reasons why very few people respond well to fear in the long run.

Another example of someone using anger inappropriately involves David, who was going through a bitter divorce. He remembered calling his ex-wife bad names in counseling. He said she was greedy and a bad mother. During the process David actually stole some of her belongings that were worth a few thousand dollars and sold them for a few hundred, because he wanted to get even with her and this was his way of doing it. So where did David's anger come from? What was the source of his anger? As we examined David's history it became apparent that he had difficulty accepting the divorce and the finality of his marriage. He was really grieving the loss of the ideal of having a family consisting of a wife and two children.

During our several months together in counseling David began to process his feelings more and more. He had grown up very lonely and devoted his life to his work. He had put his head in the sand and had tunnel vision, seeing only his work. That was the way that he showed his love to his wife and kids. He would put in long hours at work and was happy with the paycheck he brought home. The more we discussed David's feelings it became apparent that he had difficulty mourning the huge loss of support that his wife and children provided for him. Further examination of his authentic feelings revealed that David didn't treat his ex-wife Beth very well during their marriage. He often ordered her around in front of their children and would not listen to her feelings. David would get upset and mad at Beth for not following his directives regarding the development of their children. He would shout across the room in the presence of the children, "I'm mad and angry as hell that you did not do the kid's laundry!" This put fear into the hearts of Beth and the children. With ECT, David was able to recognize that he had a sense of loss around his wife and children. He began to honor his feelings and change his vocabulary. He started to use statements like, "I feel grief when my feelings are not respected," or, "I feel a sense of loss when the children don't feel that I am respected." Deep down, David began to change his behaviors that were causing him grief and loss. He began to show Beth and the children more respect also.

In short, ECT therapy helped David become more aware of the reasons for his loss of his wife. He saw that the damaged family keepsakes, worth thousands of dollars were really just an extension of the many different ways that David used poor choices to communicate his feelings towards his wife.

When David finally came to see me, he had been in a new relationship for a year or so and we were able to highlight his poor communication and anger problems with some degree of success. His new relationship was starting out stronger and it seemed to be lasting because he was becoming more authentic with his feelings. One of the key points of Emotional Core Therapy is to take responsibility for all of our actions. David had freely entered into his marriage with Beth and it did not end well because he had never truly learned to authentically process his feelings. Careful attention to detail showed that David had to recognize that his anger had negatively affected his wife. If you truly hurt somebody and are sorry you apologize afterwards and find ways to make sure that it doesn't happen again. You do these things because you see the grief and fear that other people are feeling and you respond by changing your behavior. This is something that you do because they are human and you want to be close to them.

This is another example where complete recovery did not occur. A person who wants to release guilt, which is often another word for loss or grief, will make amends properly. David made strides, but found it difficult to truly make amends to his ex-wife. By not doing so David increased the chance that he may act inappropriately again.

As he thought more about this issue of making amends for past mistakes and shortcomings, David started to realize that this was also a key tenet of his Christian faith. Though he hadn't been the most devout follower of Christ his entire life, David enjoyed reading the Bible and always found comfort in its clear teachings about God's unfathomable mercy and forgiveness.

While David moved along in the process of ECT, one day he visited a local Christian bookstore. He found a book that went right to the heart of the issue and taught him that Jesus was never condemning when it came to a person's past actions, but He didn't condone them either. For example, with the woman who was guilty of adultery, Jesus forgave her but then added, "go and sin no more." The message, David learned in this book, was to not only stop the negative behavior but to replace it with positive ways of living. He needed to become more sensitive to the needs of others and careful with the words he chose when addressing them. Daily he began praying to Jesus for the wisdom to do so, and soon he started to feel as though his prayers were being answered. David's struggles with anger didn't disappear overnight, but by sticking with ECT and re-embracing prayer more strongly than he had in many years, his life steadily started changing for the better.

As therapists we are trained to look for growth. David did grow and learn and perhaps he will pick up more from counseling in the future. David's case highlights some of the limitations of Emotional Core Therapy or any therapy because the client has to be committed to the process. Some clients want to learn all that they can to get better. If ECT was learning the alphabet, some clients would want to learn from A to Z, while others would only want to learn A through P. Therapy has to be supportive of each client no matter what state of life they are in.

Another example of a client with anger issues who learned about it from ECT was a man named Victor. He had come to the United States with his wife Tatiana more than fifteen years ago. They were both well-educated and originally from Eastern Europe, and they had three young children together. Victor was a devout Christian and his religious beliefs were an important aspect of his life. He worked very long hours and was often extremely fatigued when he arrived home. His wife Tatiana had sacrificed her career to be a homemaker. Victor often felt guilty for yelling at his wife. He would call her names, devalue her role as a mother and belittle her in front of the children. He told me, "I really don't know why I get so angry at Tatiana, I love her so very much, but I just can't help myself." When we examined their relationship at a deeper level, we found that Victor would use his role as the breadwinner in the family to have power over Tatiana and boss her around in front of the children. As Tatiana became more cognizant of her adopted country, she began to build more relationships in the United States and felt less alone and isolated. She became more outspoken and assertive about her need to be respected. Tatiana would often talk to her friends and they basically told her not to put up with her husband's tirades any longer.

Victor on the other hand, had very few friends other than work companions. As we examined his support system it became clear that he had no one to talk to after work, except his wife and children. Over the course of several months, we started the process of releasing Victor's feelings. He had never been able to tell anyone about how he felt deep inside, especially how fearful he felt. Oftentimes he was hurt and disappointed by his wife's demands for him to do household work. He had been taught when he was young that it was not manly to be bossed around by a woman at home. He got angry when Tatiana would boss him around in front of his boys. He always wanted to show her who was boss and he felt that he had to swear and yell at her to make her stop.

Of course, the anger that Victor displayed towards Tatiana only pushed them further apart. How can you love someone and be so angry at the same time? He truly wanted to improve his relationship with his wife and be a role model for his children. Victor was a very successful businessman and quite talented so he was highly motivated to change. Throughout his counseling in ECT, Victor began to heal his relationship with his wife. He realized that he needed more feedback and began to look for more male friends outside of the home. This way he wouldn't be a burden for Tatiana to be his only companion. When he had more friends, he was able to authentically share how he was feeling. He could share his deeper feelings of loss and grief.

One place Victor was able to make new friendships with like-minded people was at his local church, where he attended services. He learned through his faith and through ECT that building supportive friendships would help him. Thus, he began to strike up conversations with some of the men and soon became good friends with a few.

Moreover, learning ECT brought a new fervency and poignancy to Victor's prayer life. He now began to pray several times throughout the day. ECT taught Victor to process his emotions and cleanse his soul all day long. As the Holy Spirit worked within him, it helped Victor to stay true to his God, to himself and to the promises and commitments that he had made to his wife and family.

In therapy, Victor was coming to understand that being compassionate and merciful were key components in ECT. From the teachings of his preacher at the church, and through Victor's personal reading of the Bible, he gained a deeper understanding of mercy and compassion as two of the most beautiful attributes of God as well. In fact, the entire earthly mission of Jesus was about His mercy for the world, which He expressed for all time by His sacrifice on the cross. John 3:16 says: "For God so loved the world, that he gave his only Son, that whoever believes in him should not perish but have eternal life." That famous verse made Victor realize that, when it came to his anger, it was indeed quite possible for him to forgive others, and to forgive himself too.

This successful and strong businessman now began to see how he needed help. He no longer wanted to live a life of loneliness with no friends and have his family not like him because of his anger. Over time, Victor would recognize that he would need to work as hard as he could on being authentic with his feelings, just as Tatiana was doing her best to care for the family. In addition to seeing a counselor, he began to learn to feel comfortable with his own feelings. He also came to recognize that being lonely was something that he could change.

The goal of Emotional Core Therapy as with any therapy is to bring autonomy to the client. Victor was very comfortable identifying his feelings in therapy, but it's not enough just to do it in therapy, it has to become a part of your everyday life. The more you have support and friends the less you will be alone. This helped Victor to identify and understand that his displays of anger were really expressions of loss and grief. He began to monitor his feelings of anger each day. Every time he would start to feel angry he would ask himself, what am I losing? What am I grieving? Victor learned to pay attention to his body's symptoms. He would monitor how his muscles would tense up when he became angry and then try to calm things down through quiet relaxation techniques.

We worked with Victor's previous history to find ways for him to relax and release his feelings. He decided to join a health club where they had Pilates, yoga, and weightlifting, the kinds of things he had done in his past to relax. He also made time for himself each day to meditate and daydream, and he began to use journaling and writing to release his feelings. He felt very comfortable with writing as a vehicle to release the toxic pain of loss, so he even went a step further. Victor wrote down in a timeline all of the events in his marriage with Tatiana that cased him excess anger. We then examined each situation to see what it was that he was actually grieving. Over time (now writing his journal on a daily basis), Victor began to release his feelings in an authentic and healthy manner, and he started to feel more comfortable with himself. All of these techniques worked to improve his communication style, and in turn, his relationship with Tatiana.

Through our ECT sessions, we were beginning to understand the types of events that triggered him "blowing up" at Tatiana. We then examined each situation to see what was the underlying loss that he was feeling. By doing this, he was able to use ECT to change his life. Every time he got angry, he saw that there was another way to process his feelings. Victor was able to improve his relationship with Tatiana as he became better at recognizing his authentic feelings of loss. He realized that he needed more friends to balance his life and give him support for what he was going through with his demanding job along with his wife and three kids when he got home. Another benefit of having more supportive friends was that he became more balanced in his life which made his transition into his role as a husband and father easier. Emotional Core Therapy is about being human, and staying human. No one is ever too rich or important so that they can afford to deny their authentic self.

Over many years of doing therapy, I am constantly reminded of the humanness of all of us. In my private practice setting, I usually don't work with the serious or profoundly emotionally disturbed. Yet I do have clients who come to me with a wide range of mental health conditions. Some clients who seek treatment have been classified or diagnosed in their past as having Attention Deficit Disorder, Bipolar Disorder, Narcissistic Disorder and Obsessive Disorder. Others have sought treatment for self-mutilation issues such as cutting themselves. Some clients have suffered sexual trauma and sexual dysfunction issues. In my experience, ECT can help a broad spectrum of these types of mental health issues. Why? ECT utilizes core techniques that are common to most humans. For example, who has not suffered feelings of loss or fear? Who cannot benefit from learning various relaxation techniques? When would learning how to release feelings be detrimental to a client?

What I have found is that on rare occasions, I utilize several different techniques (not mentioned in the ECT book) for clients that have more severe personality problems. This is primarily because of resistance to change. Oftentimes you need a variety of psychological techniques to help the more resistant client to grow. In many cases, more energy and focus is needed to bring about positive outcomes with clients who are suffering serious mental health issues. Serious cases of depression, anxiety, and anger would likely benefit from a similar approach for the same reason. Any psychological technique that can successfully release emotions is helpful in treatment. ECT is very inclusive of other therapy approaches that can release emotions such as EMDR, biofeedback, hypnosis, art therapy, to name a few, Unfortunately, mentioning these would go beyond the scope of this book. I would like to point out that common everyday relaxation techniques like yoga and Pilates can be used with ECT to relax.

One of my favorite movies about hope and optimism is "The Shawshank Redemption." The main character in the movie never gave up hope about getting out of prison. His love of life was so strong that he never gave up on his dream to live his life in freedom. His will was so strong that he spent years and years chiseling rock inside his jail cell. I would like our readers to feel the same way about life. Life is so precious, why not live every day to its fullest. For this prisoner it was a life or death attitude and he chose to live – therefore he chose a way to escape out of prison.

ECT provides such a path by allowing us to relinquish toxic pain and negative energy. Remember the rudderless rowboat? What kind of rowboat would you prefer to float around in? One with water seeping in the sides and slowing the boat down? Or one that glides effortlessly through the water?

Let's go back to our client, Victor, who has feelings of anger. He also feels guilty for having his "spout" of anger. As we learned earlier, guilt is really a form of grief. It comes from mourning or grieving the self in relation to hurting another human being. We all "feel guilty" from time to time. Why? It is human nature to accidentally hurt other human beings. Let's look at this using an everyday example. Accidentally closing (or slamming) a door on someone. Nearly all of us have raced through a door, not looked behind us, and oops, the door gets shut on the next person entering the room. We feel terribly guilty. With ECT, we become increasingly in touch with our inner self. We learn to honor our feelings. When we honor our feelings, they become much easier to release. The goal of ECT is to release our four authentic feelings when they enter your mind and body. Thus, it gets a lot simpler to cleanse the soul. A clean soul is the only way you can have a rudderless rowboat.

If you shut the door on someone, next time you hold the door open. By holding the door open, you eliminate the chance for further guilt (otherwise known as the authentic feeling of grief).

One of the beautiful results of learning ECT is that no one gets a free ride in life if they aspire to stay healthy and human. Just as you can't shut the door on people without guilt, you can't kill, steal, or harm someone else, without feeling guilty (having a sense of loss) also. Why? The feelings of loss will stay inside you and not be released. Remember, the key point of ECT is to live in a meditative and relaxed state of being. In order to do ECT properly one has to monitor and release all four authentic feelings on a daily basis. Being stuck in a state of grief can be very debilitating.

Using slang words for this state of being is not hard to envision. We have all heard the phrase to describe a man who has a consistently angry personality: "What an asshole!" If they were describing a woman who is always yelling at others they might say: "What a bitch!" The phase of being angry all the time like someone described as an "asshole" or "bitch" is a very unhealthy state! That's because, not only are they unable to release their feelings, they are also not even being authentic. If they were authentic, they would be able to grieve, which is a healthier place to be emotionally. When you grieve, at least you can move towards a state of eventual peacefulness and tranquility.

Earlier in the book we discussed how you could gauge someone's success in learning Emotional Core Therapy. The more you can learn and acquire the steps of the ECT flowchart the more confident you will feel about yourself. For religious and non-religious people alike, Step Eight, using meditation, is something that you can practice at various times throughout the day. For people of faith, Step Eight can be an ideal way to stay in touch with God continuously, allowing you the peace of mind and tranquility that is so crucial as you incorporate ECT more and more into your daily life.

This book is not about becoming a leader, gaining fame or fortune. Most of the people who assume high levels of responsibility also have high levels of stress (otherwise known as fear). They have excessive fear because they have too many responsibilities and too many tasks.

I want my clients to have power, and to be able to handle their responsibilities without excessive fear or stress. ECT allows clients to get a grasp on what they can and can't handle as far as work and family stress is concerned. Oftentimes, when someone is overly fearful or stressed, anger comes out. The more you become comfortable with the ECT process, the less chance you will become angry. That's because you learn to process your feelings better. Since anger is not an authentic feeling anyway, there becomes less of a need to use anger. Emotionally healthy people can express feelings of sadness, just as readily as feelings of joy. The point is, they are being true to themselves, which is precisely what makes them emotionally healthy in the first place.

ECT Flow Chart

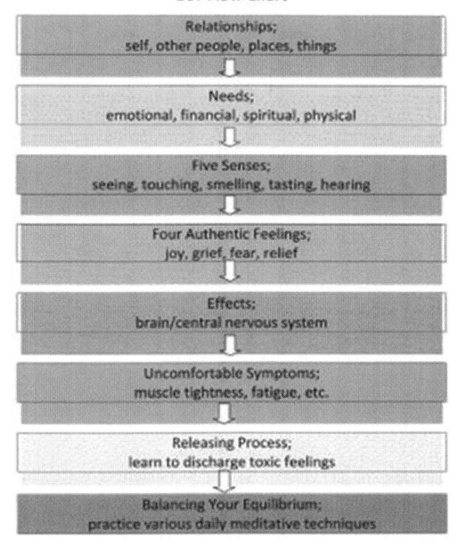

Relationships;
self, other people, places, things

⬇

Needs;
emotional, financial, spiritual, physical

⬇

Five Senses;
seeing, touching, smelling, tasting, hearing

⬇

Four Authentic Feelings;
joy, grief, fear, relief

⬇

Effects;
brain/central nervous system

⬇

Uncomfortable Symptoms;
muscle tightness, fatigue, etc.

⬇

Releasing Process;
learn to discharge toxic feelings

⬇

Balancing Your Equilibrium;
practice various daily meditative techniques

List Five Relationships / Events That Have Caused You Anger (Which Is A Reaction To Grief)

a) Getting cut off in traffic

b) Someone telling you to "shut up"

1)

2)

3)

4)

5)

NOTES:

List Five Ways That Allow You To Appropriately Process Your Anger (Which Is A Reaction To Grief)

a) I feel sad when you demand my time and energy without saying thank you.

b) I am hurt (another word for grief) that you borrow my money without paying me back.

1)

2)

3)

4)

5)

NOTES:

Symptoms Of Anger

Feeling hot and flushed

Racing heartbeat

Tension in shoulders and neck

Feeling agitated

List Five Of Your Own Symptoms Of Anger

    1)

    2)

    3)

    4)

    5)

    NOTES:

CHAPTER FIVE
Using ECT to Help Couples

As we begin to discuss how Emotional Core Therapy can help couples, I want to highlight an important reason why nearly everyone would benefit from using ECT. In doing so, let's draw upon an analogy that I used at the beginning of the book. Consider something as simple as putting on a jacket on a cold and blustery day. Most every child knows that to protect themselves from the cold, one has to put on layers of clothes to keep warm. It is something we all learn at a young age. This is the same dynamic that we are doing with our feelings. Harmful feelings of fear and loss can cause harm and danger to one's body in much the same way that a snowy and wintry day can adversely affect a person dressed only in a T-shirt and shorts. ECT is a form of self-care that has as a desired effect the reduction of toxic pain. The goal of this book is to make the reader so familiar with the process that they can use it any time, just like one uses a winter jacket.

At the beginning of the book the above paragraph may not have meant much sense to the reader. Why? At that early stage we had not covered any of the numerous relationship topics that cause one stress (debilitating feelings such as fear and grief). Now that we are near the end of the book this analogy makes more sense and begins to hit home. That's because most of us can relate somehow to the awful stresses of daily life that we have reviewed such as death, divorce, job or financial loss, etc. We have not only hammered home the concept of "relationships causing stress" but we have also provided solutions.

Back in that early part of the book we had also discussed how ECT can help in the often mentally intense sport of golf. One of the concepts I help golfers understand is that each shot is a separate relationship. Therefore, it is important to process your authentic feelings after each shot and remain in a peaceful state before you focus on your next shot. Let's take a look at this for a professional player who is playing a typical hole on a course. He will hit his drive out into the fairway. That is one shot and one relationship. Whatever experience he feels on this shot, he needs to process those feelings. In this case, he is happy with his shot so he has moments of joy. He experiences joy and releases those feelings by looking at the trees and water around him. He gets relaxed again and then prepares for his next shot in the fairway. This time he hits a poor shot into the heavy grass around the green, called the "rough". Our golfer is sad for a few minutes, but learns to release the feelings properly by processing his thoughts with his caddie. He then prepares for his next shot, which is called a chip. His ball lies deep down in the grass so he has some excess fear in his mind prior to the shot. He appropriately pays attention to his feelings of fear and changes his routine to accommodate the tough "lie or slope" of the grass. He then plays the shot and hits a nice shot near the hole. He is quite "relieved" as he now has an easy putt to get his par and do well on the hole. His relief comes from ending a fearful event or relationship.

In my experience, golfers are some of the most stable professional athletes out there. Why? Golf requires not only power but finesse and a soft touch. The game also is filled with human emotions of fear and grief every round. You cannot take drugs or be unstable and be a high performing golfer for a prolonged period of time.

Whether it is on the golf course, or in any other aspect of life, ECT is about gaining the power and independence to choose a healthy lifestyle. It is a viable solution to fighting debilitating feelings of fear and loss because of its exacting nature. All stress comes from entering and leaving relationships. The root cause of stress is moving towards relationships that we like or dislike. Most relationships require us to meet demands. To keep things simple, we can categorize these into four areas: emotional, financial, spiritual, and physical. Using our five senses (hearing, touching, seeing, tasting, and smelling) we feel one of four ways: joyful, sad, fearful, or relieved. These four feelings can cause our mind and body various levels of discomfort. We have to release these foreign feelings to reach our normal state of relaxation/comfort. Relaxation and comfort need to be reached on a daily basis so we can continually identify foreign feelings (joy, grief, fear, and relief) and deal with them appropriately.

Although the above paragraph is technical in nature, it is important to highlight. That's because some readers are more technical and science based than others. Also, there is a logical sequence to stress and its treatment. Since this book is psycho educational in nature, the reader can go back to this technically written paragraph to gauge his comprehension of the ECT process.

Indeed, I purposely wrote this technical chapter near the end of the book to lessen the fear of the reader. We all learn sequential and technical concepts in life to help aid our development. Examples include a mechanic learning how to repair a motor. A carpenter building a house. A nurse learning how to properly dispense medication. All of the above careers require education and training and rely on learning a sequence of concepts. ECT is no different, and it can be easy to learn. All you need is will and time.

A therapist often acts like a parent figure to his clients. Ask yourself, why do Mom and Dad always remind their children to dress warm during the winter? Protection. You can get sick and be subjected to long term damage when you are out in the cold for long periods of time without adequate protection. Emotional Core Therapy is my way of protecting humans from the inevitable harm that accompanies the arrival of debilitating stress. Whether you like it or not, you will suffer fear and loss in your life. In fact, most of us will have at least some minor irritation on a daily or weekly basis. Looking at the global economic problems that have evolved over the past few years it is quite obvious that many people have suffered greatly from traumatic states of fear and grief.

The real question is why not protect ourselves from this "harmful cold weather" known as stress. It seems to me that the answer is education. People realize that emotional trauma is a national epidemic but no one knows how to fix the problem. When I see the hundreds of psychology books for sale that take an advanced degree to understand, I see more clearly why a solution has not been found. There needs to be a self-help book that every literate person can read. To that extent, I have tried at great lengths to keep this ECT book reader friendly. Even nonreaders can comprehend ECT if they have someone that can teach them the process.

As we begin this chapter on couples we will again see how ECT can bring "joy" to one's life by enhancing a relationship with a loved one. Nearly all of us know the story of Romeo and Juliet. They had deep and eternal love. It seemed like the two lovebirds never failed to keep the spark or chemistry going in their relationship, no matter what difficulties came between them. The only problem with this love tragedy is that it is not very realistic. It is young love – but what if they had survived to live many more years together? Most of us have conflicts and problems with our love relationships. Since we are imperfect human beings, how can we not? Yet ECT shows us how people can make a realistic partnership better by using better communication patterns.

Before I discuss a few cases where Emotional Core Therapy helped couples navigate through their lives, I want to mention some basic thoughts regarding the commitment that a marital or couples' relationship offers to a person. First and foremost is the hope of everyone that begins a relationship with a partner that the relationship will provide support. In the modern day world with increasing life spans into the 80s and 90s, many people will choose to remain single for a period of time. I see lots of people in therapy that seem very happy with their lives being single. There are even benefits to being single for a period of time. You get to know to learn and love yourself without having the demands of a partner on a daily basis. Still, others recognize that they have a better chance of getting all of their needs met through a committed relationship. Since ECT deals with authentic feelings, there is no difference in treatment of couples of various races or cultures. Emotional, financial, spiritual, and physical needs as we already know vary from person to person. I've discovered the benefits of focusing on authentic feelings in a relationship takes away from biases of both the client and therapists.

In this chapter we begin to see more clearly what brings us stress in our relationships with our husband or wife. It is the "needs" and "demands" that each partner brings to the relationship that cause us to have one of the four authentic feelings. In our ECT Flowchart, we see that needs are broken down to four areas. These are emotional, financial, spiritual, and physical. We have organized needs into these four areas because they provide a simple structure for us to understand what causes us stress. There are literally millions of stresses in relationships. To discuss the various needs of ourselves and others would overwhelm the reader. So for the sake of simplicity we break them down into one of four areas.

Let's take a look at how a simple relationship can be viewed in this manner. We are driving our car when a policeman waves us to stop temporarily to direct traffic. In this case, the relationship with the policeman required a physical need to be addressed. We had to stop our trip temporarily before moving on.

A relationship with our husband or wife is much more demanding as far as various needs being met. A wife may have many more needs to be met from her husband during the day, including things such as doing the dishes, walking the dog, going to the store, cutting the lawn, etc. The list goes on and on.

The aspect of the four areas of needs being met (emotional, financial, spiritual, and physical) as a step of ECT is really more of a guideline. It is meant to bring a clearer focus of what really causes us discomfort in relationships. Just as we won't spend a great deal of time discussing the five senses (hearing, touching, smelling, tasting, and seeing), we also will skim over the various needs that have to be met in relationships. That's because both happen to us most of the time automatically, whether we like it or not.

Emotional Core Therapy is about being human and to honor one's self, which in turn requires us to honor others. For this reason, we cannot just focus on what happens to our self in a relationship. Inevitably, we have to respond in some form to others too. From time to time, I hope the reader glances at the ECT flowchart. Over time the flow and sequence of events will become clearer and clearer.

Earlier in the book we discussed how ECT can make a thunderstorm feel like a drizzle. To explain our analogy, we used an example where we discussed how a teacher that supervises four children has an easier task than one who supervises 150. Discussing the four levels of needs (emotional, financial, spiritual, and physical) can be also viewed in this manner. We can usually sort out the millions of various needs required of us to be broken down into one of these four areas.

The first couple I want to discuss is Ted and Sue. This couple in their early fifties came to my office because of marital strife and discord. They had been fighting with each other for several months and now the wife had begun to contemplate divorce. Ted wasn't listening to many of her concerns. Sue was stressed out all the time because they had barely enough money to survive. Ted spent their money foolishly and now they were down to nearly their last penny. As they examined the wife's history, it became apparent that they had met in an unusual fashion. Her husband had a successful job at a company where Sue had worked on a voluntary basis. She was very attracted to his power and position within this company as he was president. Sue saw Ted give powerful speeches and saw him being admired by people throughout the company. He seemed to always be able to captivate a room full of people with his charisma. Ted would notice the glaze in Sue's eyes while in work alone. One thing led to another and soon Ted and Sue began to have a love affair. Both of them decided to make a decision to announce that they were going to divorce their spouses and get married.

Unfortunately for their plans to live happily ever after, the company found out and fired Ted. Soon Sue left her volunteer position and Ted had to find new work. He had to switch his line of work because of the bad public relations that stain would cause in the community. Ted's new position was at a steep decline in pay and held little prestige so he lost some of his power too.

For Sue, she had envisioned a financially secure life for her and her children. Both Ted and Sue had children with their previous spouses and there was some conflict there because of the newness of their relationship. Ted also had to pay child support to his ex-wife, and soon Sue had to go into her savings to pay the bills. After being married for five years most of Sue's savings were depleted and they were living paycheck to paycheck instead of enjoying a luxury lifestyle. That was the point when they came to my office.

When we examine Sue's statement of emotional pain regarding finances, we focused on her authentic feelings of grief. Sue was grieving the ideal of a financially secure relationship and a perfect marriage without a lot of turmoil. In addition, she had a lot of fear regarding her future, how she could protect and take care of herself and her kids. The focus of the treatment with both Sue and Ted was to highlight the authentic feelings of fear and loss that Sue faced. By listening to Sue processing her feelings it started to become apparent that there was more than one way Sue felt loss and fear. She was also grieving the loss of a new home, the happy relationship and most of all, Sue was grieving the loss of a man who cared and listened to her.

As we discussed Sue's fears with Ted in therapy, it became apparent that Ted had difficulty emotionally connecting with women. He had felt estranged from his ex-wife while they were married, and in fact that is why he started an affair. Now in this new relationship he also began to escape the responsibilities of his commitment to his new spouse, Susan.

Over the years, though both had been raised in secular homes, Ted and Sue had developed an interest in Christianity. Both of them had always been rather spiritually curious, and they had together attended an outdoor "tent revival" one weekend and the couple felt drawn by the messages of faith, hope and love that they heard from the various preachers. Soon afterwards they started incorporating these Christian concepts into their lives. They agreed that it would fit in well with what they were learning from ECT, and they were determined to combine both approaches moving forward.

During our course of couples' therapy, we made a list of what each needed at different levels (emotional, financial, spiritual and physical) from each other. We discussed on a weekly basis, the efforts to meet each partner's needs. We tried to spend equal time in therapy stressing each person's needs, and not being just one sided. So we spent half the time on Sue and half on Ted. When couples first meet they are highly motivated to meet each other's needs. There is a great deal of lust and chemistry taking place. I tried to let Sue and Ted know that that eagerness and excitement that they felt when they were first attracted to each other is what they need to feel today. In other words, people have to work just as hard years into the marriage as they did when they first met each other.

As couples go through months and years of living together, sometimes they forget to stay motivated and committed to the process of supporting their partner. Successful relationships are the result of mature couples meeting each other's needs. I often tell my clients, the more a man stays committed in a relationship, the more he acquires feminine attributes and traits. The more a woman stays committed to a man in a relationship, the more masculine traits she acquires. With Ted and Sue, it was not hard to see the dilemma they faced in their relationship. Ted was used to relying on his status of power, money and charisma to satisfy a woman's needs. Yet this was not what Sue needed at all. Ted had difficulty really paying attention to the emotional feeling of loss that Sue was displaying on a daily basis. He also had difficulty relating to her excessive fear. As he said one time in counseling, Ted continually tried to hide himself in work to escape the authentic feeling of grief that Sue had in their relationship. We sought ways to help Ted change this. He recalled that the Bible instructs followers of Jesus to "put on the mind of Christ." This helped Ted to make the adjustments that he knew were necessary for their relationship.

Fortunately for Sue, she was willing to assert herself with her feelings. Sue felt empowered by being in therapy and did not want to lose this chance to feel better. Both Sue and Ted were not getting any younger and they decided to make the relationship work. They both realized that another divorce would wreak havoc in both themselves and their children's lives. So they both spent time working hard on making sure each other's feelings were heard, in the authentic feelings of fear, grief, loss and relief. As part of this effort, they agreed to read the Bible and pray together daily. They especially latched onto scriptural passages where Jesus offered words of hope and encouragement for those who will let go of their fears and apprehension, and place their trust in Him and follow Him. A prime example would be John 16:33, where Jesus said: "I have told you these things, so that in me you may have peace. In this world you will have trouble. But take heart! I have overcome the world."

Emotional Core Therapy points out how various things come into and out of our lives and profoundly affect our peace of mind. It lined up well with the couple's Christian beliefs, and was successful with both Ted and Sue as they were able to grasp the concepts fairly easily. Ted began to help Sue grieve properly and started to hold and hug her more while in therapy as well as when they were home. Ted and Sue also made a budget together and they worked on their finances weekly because that was a big concern for them and they began to look forward to solving their financial issues and lowering their costs and expenses each month. Ted also started seeking a higher paying job in another company. Over time Sue and Ted were able to rekindle the spark that they had when they first met. For Sue's part, it was important to give her credit for being true to herself and her feelings of fear and grief. Sue had felt awful at the beginning of therapy and she was determined to rid herself of toxic feelings of loss and grief. As we examined Ted's needs, we saw that he was truly happy in his relationship except for not being able to please Sue. He really didn't have a lot of excess needs himself that needed to be met so we were able to focus a lot on alleviating Sue's pain.

Over the course of several months Sue was able to process her feelings better and release her pain. Some of the things that cause couple's pain, such as poor finances and lack of communication began to dissipate and end. They concluded therapy after seven months, feeling more optimistic about the future.

Emotional Core Therapy can give hope to a couple in therapy, as it matches authentic feelings with the needs of partners. Most couples can learn a process of being authentic in their feelings by using ECT. When ECT is used with couples, it can bring them closer together and they both can learn at the same time the different techniques of ECT. In other words, they both can help each learn it in addition to the therapist helping them. As a relationship builds, ECT is also helpful in building autonomy for both partners. They both can work on finding peace for themselves, which is important for a healthy relationship. When you have peace in your life and you work on it every day, you start to work on vitality and vigor which is basically a sign of power. We want both partners in therapy to have as much power as they want and to feel as vibrant as possible. That only comes from being emotionally balanced.

With Emotional Core Therapy, the "process" is the product. We are teaching a new way of approaching life. Sure, ECT takes time to learn, but the long-term benefits are very high. If stress is the number one killer of humans, then decreasing your stress will lengthen your life. The key to this "process" is (as we mentioned earlier) externalizing your feelings, versus internalizing your feelings. Remember how we discussed how feelings get released? It can happen anywhere! It is not likely that this will only happen in a therapist's office. Feelings can be released while sunbathing on a beach, dancing to music, doing meditation, etc. That is why with ECT we place an emphasis on both meditation and relaxation exercises. Both meditation and relaxation techniques have a likelihood of releasing toxic feelings. It is important, once again, to draw a distinction between meditation and "relaxation" exercises. Meditation is a state of being that allows one to daydream, reflect, and has a free flowing nature about how your mind eases from topic to topic. Realistically, with relaxation techniques some cognition or effort is needed with the mind. Earlier in the book we discussed gardening as a relaxation technique. When you garden, you nonetheless have to think of the steps needed to correctly grow your plants. Still, basking under the sun alone, and in nature can be the perfect way to release thoughts and feelings. With both meditation and relaxation techniques, you can slow down the central nervous system, which is our goal with ECT.

Imagine two of your favorite movie stars, one male and one female. Both have warm smiles and are emotionally balanced on screen, with a calm disposition, yet both are full of life and vigor. Both portray emotionally healthy personalities and are well liked. Why? When we look at them we see engaging figures who are empathetic and well-liked by others, and I think what draws people to such stars are their "approachable" personalities.

Movie stars are mature adult figures who portray a zest for life. That is what the benefits of ECT can allow. You keep control of your senses. Your sense of humor, love of music, optimism for the future are all possible if you can live a life of honoring your sense of self. You keep your vitality for life as you look forward to healthier relationships.

Now let's go back to you, the reader. I am not saying I want everyone to act like a movie star. Quite the contrary. With ECT, we recognize the uniqueness and individual beauty of all people. What I hope for with all my clients is to have them obtain vitality and passion for life. In other words, power! I am not opposed to wealth, powerful positions of authority, etc. In fact, I hope that all of my clients do their best in all aspects of their life.

We discussed earlier in the book what makes for a healthy relationship. Certain components like honesty, openness, and reciprocity, are all parts of a healthy relationship. Whether it be a marriage, friendship, work assignment, etc. all healthy relationships have these core components. Examining each relationship through the eyes of Emotional Core Therapy, we see that healthy relationships honor the four authentic feelings of joy, grief, fear, and relief. A healthy relationship recognizes that the individual may need space to relax and have time for himself/herself. When you can finally begin to understand this key point of ECT, you can begin to have "real and authentic" power. Power you can count on long-term. Relationships that last a long time.

The second couple I would like to highlight is a young couple named Jeff and Kim who decided to live together before they were married. Both were very energetic and optimistic young people. They were both successful at work and had a great group of friends. Both were very popular in the office and their respective workplaces. They were both quite attracted to each other and obviously very committed to each other. So what could possibly be wrong that such a vibrant and strong young couple would need to see a marital therapist? Why would they blow up and get so mad at each from time to time? How would ECT be able to help them?

The main issue that Jeff and Kim faced was that when they disagreed on something it would always result in a loud blowout fight. They could be very affectionate with each other one minute and swearing and yelling at each other the next. They were both extremely perplexed as to why this occurred and they didn't realize it themselves. Jeff and Kim were obviously very popular and successful irrespective of each other. Prior to their relationships both of them were happy go lucky individuals, both were athletic in high school and hung around with the in crowd. They each had supportive families and were financially secure. Both were upstanding, law abiding citizens with good intentions for their lives. At the core of the couple's dispute was the problem that being a couple means that you have to share. You have to compromise with the other person's point of view.

As a therapist I would hope that my young clients indeed, all my clients, would be as optimistic and energetic as Jeff and Kim were in their everyday lives. The real problem with Jeff and Kim's relationship was that they jumped in very quickly to becoming lovers with each other. When they lived separately they yearned for each other. The attraction was so powerful that they leapt into getting an apartment and began to live as a couple. Instead of spending weekends apart from each other and missing each other they were now together each day. As I explained to the young couple they just needed to find a healthy balance of time spent with each other and apart from each other. Over the years I've found that regardless of age, sex or ethnicity, all couples have to work on having an emotionally healthy self, separate from a relationship with their partner. A good relationship exists when both individuals respect themselves but also support the process that a true partnership provides.

As a metaphor, I used two magnets with opposite energies. When two magnets are far apart they seek each other out. But when the magnets are too close they repel. This is just like couples do when they initially meet. When two people are too close together they repel. And they will wait for each other. It would be ideal to have a magnetic energy that was perfectly in balance all the time. But that is not realistic of life. As ECT tells us, all relationships are either growing toward us or moving away. These relationships evoke feelings in us such as joy, fear, grief and relief. All young couples including Kim and Jeff are excited and motivated to begin a relationship with their new partner. Why? It's a chance for joy. What is joy? Happiness and pleasure. We all want that authentic feeling and we are trained as kids to pursue it. You are told to save money in a piggy bank when you are little. Why? You will be able to buy things that you enjoy when you are older. Study hard in school. Why? You'll be able to get a job when you are older so you can buy new things. Or live a life with good resources.

Young people like to watch romance or love movies. Why? Everyone hopes to meet Prince Charming or a perfect girl. Eternal joy, however, is a myth that in most cases is broken quite quickly once couples start living together. Healthy relationships are usually the result of two adults committed to working on a relationship. The key is the word "work," which means time. It takes work and effort to see the other person's point of view. It takes time to learn the emotional, financial, spiritual and physical needs of a partner. The healthier relationships that I see are those where both partners really appreciate the benefit of having a partner and desire to work toward making their partner happy. That's what real maturity is, a recognition that yes I could live my life single and survive every day. The reader may ask what makes somebody want to work on a relationship with a partner. The answer is really no different than a job or career. Oftentimes people are motivated to find a job because they need money. They may initially be motivated by fear of being poor and having few resources. Others may be motivated by joy; they may have so much joy in what they are doing that they make a career out of it.

Relationships with a partner are usually motivated by the same authentic feelings of joy and fear. With Kim and Jeff, it was obvious that they had a great deal of joy motivating them to be together. But the real problem with both of these young people was that they were not used to working on a relationship on a day to day level on the four aspects of emotional, financial, spiritual and physical needs. In other words, because they jumped in so quickly they had more demands placed on them and they were overwhelmed and not used to it.

With ECT we came across certain things about the relationship with Kim and Jeff. They both had to change addresses and move and this costs money. They both had to pay for a wedding and this cost money. They had to spend more time with each other each day so they had to listen to each other more. They both had different views of religion, which meant compromise. They both had different needs physically so they had to learn a great deal about each other in a short amount of time. All of this was overwhelming to them and caused an excessive amount of fear.

We also discussed Jeff and Kim's religious beliefs. Both of them had been raised as Christians, but in different denominations. Rather than letting this divide them, however, soon after becoming a couple they joined a non-denominational Christian church. It had a great atmosphere and made both of them feel welcome and at home. As they learned more about ECT, they realized that these new concepts would strengthen what they already believed as Christians. Not in accordance with any specific denominational doctrine, but perfectly in line with deeply held beliefs and practices accepted by all Christians worldwide.

When we examined Jeff and Kim's new life using Emotional Core Therapy we were able to see that they had started their relationship very quickly which led to each of them having excessive fear. Jeff was feeling afraid that he might abandon Kim because he couldn't deal with living with a woman so young in his life. He was afraid that he couldn't deal with all the drama and emotions. Kim was feeling equally fearful that she would not be able to handle all of the household chores that she felt obligated to do. She wasn't sure that she would be able to get a handle on it and take care of a man.

Over the course of several months we examined all of the four authentic feelings involved with Jeff and Kim. They were able to see that they would need to make minor adjustments and compromises for each of their needs, so that they could balance their life a little bit better. There was a reassuring feeling by both of them that they could work through their marital relationship to change their lives.

Around Easter time, the sermon in their church reminded the congregation of how Jesus had washed the feet of His disciples as a symbol of how men and women need to serve each other. What better way to serve each other than to meet each other's emotional, financial, spiritual, and physical needs? When you meet each other's needs you are growing together and building a foundation of Christian love. This holy and very lovely ideal spurred on the couple to each try to be a little less selfish and to give their partner's wants and needs precedence over their own. Not only was this emotionally and psychologically healthy, it was a very Christian way of strengthening your relationship with the person you love more than anybody else in the world.

The ECT approach was helpful with both Kim and Jeff as they were both able to recognize their individual feelings and work toward a resolution. One of the key things that they both did very well in therapy was to learn to relax and spend some time by themselves each day. This was so they could calm themselves down.

It is important to see that the releasing of feelings can happen at any time. Take for example when you are getting massaged from a kind and supportive massage therapist. I have seen examples where people can get familiar with someone and pent up toxic feelings are released. Even though massage therapists are not trained psychotherapists or counselors they still are in a situation where feelings can be released. There is no intent to do so, yet this nonetheless happens. The point is, ECT can happen in various different places. Ideally I would like everyone with emotional pain to see their nearest therapist for as long as they like, several times a week. This is not realistic for many reasons, but that's okay because sometimes people can learn to release their feelings elsewhere. Remember there is a time and a place for the release of cathartic release of feelings. One just has to use their common sense. For example, we wouldn't want someone to start screaming out about their fear of nightmares at their daughter's violin recital!

Much like learning to swim or ride a bike, learning to express one's feelings is a process. At the core of the process is externalizing our feelings versus internalizing them.

In simple terms, externalizing one's feelings means to put something outside of the mind. In other words, the release of fear or a thought. Internalizing means to incorporate within oneself. There are good things to internalize-values, ethics, homework, anything learned-however, toxic fears are unhealthy for the mind and body. These negative stored feelings are not really healthy to keep in and they cause stress. Oftentimes people who store their feelings repeatedly have body function problems such as muscular tension, hands trembling, sweating, shaking and nightmares. Not only are these feelings uncomfortable they are unhealthy.

Jeff and Kim were able to work through the major relationship changes in their lives in a short period of time because they truly saw the benefit or having a partner and the joy it could bring. ECT was helpful to both of them as they were both able to recognize their individual feelings and work toward a resolution.

A person has to be fully capable of giving in a relationship to a partner. Let's look at all four aspects of one's needs in a relationship in a hypothetical case. This case involves a very healthy young lady who was vibrant and successful and full of life. She meets someone like Jeff from our first example but in this case the man gets in a car accident soon after they get together. He has surgery, loses his job and is in a lot of pain. The point is no one can predict the future or predict how relationships will work out in the future. This is all the more reason to focus on authentic feelings as a therapist and also for our clients. As we focus more on authentic feelings we move towards a better resolution and there are less surprises and less shock in one's life. With ECT we have an equal responsibility of listening to each other's needs. Meditation and relaxation are hallmarks of emotionally healthy people. Many successful people learn to balance their workplace and family responsibilities with ways to relax. As long as one can daydream and keep reflective one can let their mind relax. It doesn't have to be sitting in a yoga position or listening to your body. There are other ways to do it.

The real reason why Emotional Core Therapy is a game changer in the field of psychology is the ability for the client to "transfer" the invaluable techniques learned in this book to new relationships. For example, when you enter ECT therapy to deal with a domineering spouse who overwhelms you to exhaustion, you learn some basic tools to protect yourself. You learn how to identify fear, feel the symptoms of fear, process those feelings, and work towards a meditative state. Once you learn a meditative state, it is easier to identify future feelings of fear with the spouse. You can then utilize techniques that you have learned to change your behavior so that you don't continue to experience these feelings over and over again.

Let's look at an example of this in simple terms. A young couple shares a small apartment together with one bathroom. The wife is used to spending an hour in the bathroom getting ready in the morning. There is only one toilet, one shower and one bathroom sink in this small apartment. So every morning when the husband, Sal, gets ready for work, he has to wait an hour to use the bathroom. After a short time in this setting, he feels hurt and disrespected by his wife. He also is very anxious about being late for work. His authentic feelings of fear and grief begin to affect Sal's central nervous system. He becomes agitated, experiences muscle tension, and starts to have rapid thoughts and be in a state of panic. He also begins to lose hope. These symptoms have to be released somehow. Sal does his ECT homework and identifies the "relationship" he has entered into that is causing him stress. He changes his behavior by discussing the issues with his wife. They negotiate alternate days to use the bathroom in the morning. Sal begins to feel empowered in the relationship, and he is able to release his authentic feelings of fear and grief in a constructive manner with his wife. He then regains his normal, peaceful and meditative state.

Now, two weeks later Sal has similar feelings of fear and grief over his co-worker parking in his parking spot at work. He utilizes the same ECT techniques he learned with his wife to combat the insensitive co-worker. What we are discussing here is a "transferable" ability. Because ECT relies on authentic feelings, which are simple and easy to learn, the client has a much better chance of utilizing his "learned behavior" with future relationships and events in his life.

One of the most important dynamics of learning Emotional Core Therapy is the wisdom to know that traumatic grief and fear can happen to anyone. Whether one is a master at ECT or just an emotionally healthy person, we all have to live in the real world where loved ones get sick, people lose their jobs and homes, etc. For this very reason, it is important to equip yourself with psychological assistance that will help you over a lifetime, and not just once. With ECT, the client is empowered by the process as he is learning it in his long-term memory. He /she will own the technique.

Therapy can be an expensive process. It can hurt to shell out dollar after dollar every time you have a serious relationship issue. Why not become your own therapist? When you have learned ECT you can transfer this skill set to all of your relationships, wherever you go, whomever you are with. This is because ECT is fundamentally sound. In the example above, the husband, Sal, has resolved the difficulty with his wife and co-worker using ECT. Now Sal can use what he has learned in other fearful events. For example, learning how to swim or hit a softball, or overcoming his fear of snakes. Fear is fear, no matter what the relationship is that is causing Sal to feel debilitated. Sure, the levels of fear may vary from dealing with a loving wife versus playing softball with friends. Sal's mind and bodily response may change also. But the science behind it does not. Over time, someone like Sal can begin to feel confident that he has more control over his life. He can steer away from more fearful and grief stricken relationships because he can sense their danger. The more he can distance himself from debilitating feelings, the more powerful he can be in life with his relationships.

A third example of how Emotional Core Therapy can help married people involves a couple named Mary and Henry. They both were in their fifties and had raised a couple of children. Henry had recently sold his successful business and was planning an early retirement. Mary had always been a stay at home mom who did volunteer work. Henry was always devoted to his work and his devotion meant that the family had a good deal of financial resources, such as a nice home and a high standard of living. For Henry, retirement meant that he could finally rest and spend his days golfing and sitting around the coffee shop with his friends. This sounded really appealing to him because he was tired of the daily grind. For Mary, retirement meant that she was able to spend time with her husband. She would also be able to do all the things she wanted to do such as shopping and vacationing.

When we began couples' therapy, Henry was resentful of change. He did not like the idea that his relationship with Henry had to change too. Before when he was a businessman she had felt alone now she demanded more from him. As we had mentioned previously, nobody can predict the future. If they were going to save their marriage, we would have to work towards making Mary happy. This meant changes to Henry's plans for retirement. In some manner Henry had to grieve the loss of retirement, playing around with his guy friends and resting. For Mary's part, she wanted to stay with Henry if he became a full partner in the marriage. Over the course of twenty-five years, Mary had become more confident in herself and her life. She was a few years younger than Henry and she had decided that if he didn't wake up and spend more time with her, she was going to divorce him. Fortunately for both Mary and Henry, the fear of divorce was a motivating factor. Henry didn't want to lose the money that he had worked so hard to earn in his career so he was willing to work hard in therapy.

Moreover, as devout Christians, they knew that their religion emphasized the importance of a good marriage, and strongly discouraged divorce. A key teaching of the Christian faith is to seek the wisdom of the Bible in all important matters, especially life changing issues such as marriage. Henry and Mary did this, and they found many verses that helped them to gain a deeper appreciation of their obligations to one another as spouses. In the very beginning of the Bible, in the Genesis account of creation, it described how God created Eve because "it was not good for the man (Adam) to be alone." Both Henry and Mary acknowledged the truth of this advice, that despite their problems they were happier together than either of them would be apart. They felt as though God was speaking to them through His Word, opening their eyes to the reality that their marriage was indeed worth saving. The longtime couple agreed to work their prayerful study of scripture into what they were trying to accomplish through their use of ECT.

As part of this process, we made a list each week of the things that Mary wanted to do and Henry worked hard towards many of these things. It was not the retirement he had envisioned. He had to grieve that loss. He had to process that and recognize that he had to alter certain circumstances of his life that involved reconnecting with his wife.

Initially he had a lot of fear about this, i.e., spending more time with Mary. For years he had avoided her during work but now he had lived with that fear and he tried to work toward overcoming it on a daily basis. This process took several months but eventually Henry discovered that doing these things for his wife was well worth the effort. In Paul's first letter to the Thessalonians, he urges Christians to give thanks for everything in their lives. Putting this teaching into practice, Henry gained a new appreciation for his wife, thanking God for her and seeing their lives together through fresh eyes for the first time in a quarter of a century.

So, as part of his new commitment, Henry would go shopping with her, he would spend time going on vacation with her and he would help her with household activities. Eventually, they began to experience a stronger, more intimate relationship and a marriage that was no longer teetering on the brink of disaster.

One of the many positive aspects of Emotional Core Therapy is the ability to simplify "psychological help" so that a large sector of the population can benefit from it and use it in their daily life. Earlier in the book we discussed the prevalence of mental health problems. Inappropriate behaviors or inadequate self-soothing techniques cause many of these problems. ECT is a learned process. It relies on using your logic to learn a sequence of steps. ECT also requires you to monitor your body on a daily basis. Most Kindergartens in the United States and around the world follow similar routines. For example, learning the alphabet and following school rules. Christianity also requires learning similar training. For example, reciting prayers and following the rules of the church. There is a track record of early intervention in our educational system. So I am optimistic of ECT helping our youth. Also, anywhere people gather in large groups, such as in the workplace, ECT can benefit with its humanistic approach. The key is making mental health a priority.

My goal is for the reader to master the ECT process by the time they finish reading the book. To further help the reader I would like to point out that the eight-step ECT flowchart is easier to master than meets the eye. Why? The first three steps happen to most of us, whether we like them or not. The first three steps are:

1. Understanding the impact that relationships have on our mind and body.
2. Understanding the needs (emotional, financial, spiritual, and physical) of people that we have a relationship with.
3. Having our five senses (hearing, touching, tasting, smelling, and seeing) prompt us to have one of the four authentic feelings.

Let's look at an example to prove our point. We hear an ambulance race past us with loud sirens blaring down the street. Whether we like it or not we have entered into a relationship that causes us to use our sense of hearing to move out of the way (moving out of the way is a physical need being required of us). For most of us, such basic tenets of ECT will not be hard to grasp. The real challenge in learning ECT is to identify which authentic feeling is being aroused by your senses. In the case of the ambulance, it is "fear". The next key learning technique is to monitor your body (a message is sent to your central nervous system almost unconsciously) and muscular skeletal system for adverse reactions and debilitating symptoms. Going further, the next key strategy is to learn to release this negative energy somehow. Finally, a diligent effort to maintain peace and relaxation is needed to remind the body of its normal state of comfort. Hence, the real challenge of learning ECT is to completely learn these four vital steps. For nearly all of us, it will take a few months at the very least to master these four techniques. This only makes sense, because we are retraining our mind and body, which takes time and effort. Nothing comes easy, but the reward of a healthy and balanced lifestyle is well worth the effort.

Once you have read this book from cover to cover, you can then assess how much knowledge you have attained learning the ECT process. If you can only recall six of the eight steps, you can then focus on learning the remaining two steps, without having to reread the whole book. For example, let's say you understand most of the book, except for understanding how the four authentic feelings are caused by relationships. What you can do is open the book to the chapter where we discuss the diagram of entering and leaving relationships

(large red and green arrows with four authentic feelings moving towards or away from relationships)

Let's return to the analogy of the rudderless rowboat one more time, to see what it is that slows a person down in life. Too much water in the rowboat will slow or stop the power. Water inside the rowboat for months and years will make even a "Mercedes" rowboat travel like a paddleboat. We can see what drains the passion out of a strong person's will. It is toxic relationships that cause one to have debilitating feelings of grief and fear for long periods of time. Remember, we can all get "stuck" in hard to deal with relationships from time to time. That is after all, what love is about. For example, your wife is fighting cancer for several years. Your husband loses his job and can't find another for a year, etc. These types of difficult relationship problems that couples face day in and day out can deplete any rowboat. The key, however, is to diligently apply all that you have learned about Emotional Core Therapy and keep working to find a resolution. Keep the faith and be relentless when it comes to making changes to your self-soothing techniques to try and stay calm.

List Five Ways A Couple Can Relax Together

A) GOING TO A SPA FOR A MASSAGE

B) GOING ON A CRUISE/SAILBOAT

1)

2)

3)

4)

5)

NOTES:

List Five Ways Your Partner Can Meet Your Emotional, Financial, Spiritual, and Physical Needs

1)

2)

3)

4)

5)

List Five Ways Your Partner Can Honor Your Four Authentic Feelings of Joy, Grief, Fear, and Relief.

1)

2)

3)

4)

5)

ECT Flow Chart

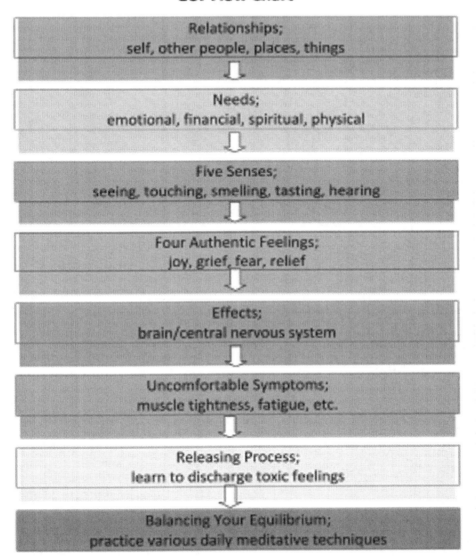

Relationships;
self, other people, places, things

⇩

Needs;
emotional, financial, spiritual, physical

⇩

Five Senses;
seeing, touching, smelling, tasting, hearing

⇩

Four Authentic Feelings;
joy, grief, fear, relief

⇩

Effects;
brain/central nervous system

⇩

Uncomfortable Symptoms;
muscle tightness, fatigue, etc.

⇩

Releasing Process;
learn to discharge toxic feelings

⇩

Balancing Your Equilibrium;
practice various daily meditative techniques

CHAPTER SIX
Using ECT to Treat Addictions

The following information will show how Emotional Core Therapy techniques can be used to treat addictions. Before reading the chapter I will give you a modern definition of the word addiction.

Addiction: Compulsive physiological and psychological need for a habit-forming substance. **The condition of being habitually or compulsively occupied with or in something. For example, someone having an addiction to shopping or fast cars.**

We hear a lot about addictions these days, and believe it or not that's a good thing. Not that they are so widespread, but that people are actually talking about them. Once upon a time, addictions of any kind were deep dark secrets that people kept buried away, never to be discussed even with close friends or family. However, times have changed. There are countless books on the subject, support groups, even television shows dedicated to the topic of addictions.

Addictions come in so many variations that it would be difficult to list all of them, as they range from alcohol to pornography to gambling and just about everything in between. The purpose of this chapter is to show you through several cases that I have treated how my Emotional Core Therapy approach can aid those suffering from addictions. Hopefully, by the time you finish reading you will understand how ECT will empower you to beat addictions while showing you a better way to cope with other aspects of life.

I like to use analogies when explaining difficult concepts. A good example of someone attempting to find happiness in being addicted to something is like "Fool's Gold". Years ago, people would search for gold only to find useless rocks that looked like real gold but were valueless. Their hardworking efforts were in vain and useless. That is the same feeling people have when they try and escape life through addictions. The escape or rush you feel from being addicted to something will not last. There is always a crash or downturn to being in an addicted state.

In Emotional Core Therapy terms, the rush you feel (the state of being addicted to something) can be seen as people attempting to find temporary or permanent joy from their addiction. Instead addicts always find the authentic feelings of fear and grief. You cause fear and grief to yourself by being an addict because the addictions never last and are often costly emotionally and financially. You often cause fear and grief to others. This may include your loved ones such as family and friends.

This chapter will get us started by briefly examining how emotional core therapy can help those suffering from any addiction. ECT allows you to not feel alone with your suffering. There are many curative factors that occur during treatment including making participants feel connected, involved, and empowered.

ECT starts with a premise that maintains that the natural state of human beings is to have a mindset that is playful, meditative, relaxed and reflective. That is where love comes from, and it is what gives human beings power. Anything that takes away from that causes you to lose your power. ECT explains the loss of power rather than simply surrendering to the addiction. You lose your sense of loving yourself because you have entered into a new relationship (with the addiction) that is highly toxic. This new relationship can possibly endanger your body and your mind. Also, you may put yourself in jeopardy with the criminal justice system. Worse yet, you can destroy your family life. A relationship with an addiction, like all relationships, is something that we enter into by choice. It is up to each individual to remain in their addicted relationship or leave it for good. As we learn how harmful and toxic our addiction is to our health, we will become motivated to make better relationship choices. Also, we will be motivated to want to leave that relationship with the addiction.

As you will learn, through ECT you will discover that you already have the power within you to overcome addiction. ECT promotes healing by making people understand that they have the power to love themselves, and to learn how to meditate and relax. That means you are not letting go of your will. Rather, you are coming to comprehend the power that you already have within you to begin moving away from the toxic relationship that you have entered into with addiction.

ECT allows us to breakdown the emotions associated with the addictive behaviors. We examine what brings us the four authentic feelings: which are joy, grief, fear and relief, and then use ECT to eliminate whatever it is that is hindering our tranquility. What is causing us pain emotionally? What grief are we trying to drown out with our addictions? What fears are we trying to suppress with drugs and other addictions? ECT offers practical tools for answering all of these important questions and more, which ultimately leads to effective treatment and recovery.

Of course, to use ECT successfully, you do need to be open and honest with your feelings, at least with yourself, and for most of us, with other people. Talking with others can help us sort out our feelings. We have to understand all of the relationships that we enter into, including our relationship with addictions. This does not happen overnight, and it can take several months to effectively learn all of the steps of ECT. It's sort of like taking on a new job; you don't understand all of the responsibilities until you've been on board for a while. So understanding the exact nature of your problems can take some time, and discussing it with others is part of the treatment.

Emotional Core Therapy is about learning to continually remind your mind that a relaxed and meditative state is a healthy lifestyle. Day in and day out we are monitoring, identifying and releasing the four authentic feelings, all of which can be numbed or harmed by addictions. Mental health, substance abuse, and addictions are complex issues that can be extremely challenging even for highly trained professionals. I want to remind readers again to notify their family physician for an appropriate referral when you begin addictions treatment.

ECT offers a streamlined and inclusive approach for overcoming all sorts of addictions. Not only that, but when you master ECT (and it's a lot easier than you may think) you will see that not only can it help you to overcome addictions, but it can also help you to live a better, more mentally stable and peaceful life in general. Remember, when you learn the ECT process you can transfer what you learn into relationship stress at work, school and home.

The first case that I would like to share with you in the addictions chapter is the case of Rebecca. Rebecca saw me for mental health and substance abuse issues for a period of seven months. Rebecca told me her troubles began several years ago when she was a senior in high school. During Rebecca's intake evaluation, we discovered a strained relationship with her father and losing contact with some close friends as they made the transition into college and the working field. Rebecca and I worked hard in therapy to deal with her addiction issues with alcohol, marijuana and a junk food diet.

I treated Rebecca using my Emotional Core Therapy flow chart. A key part of our treatment was educating Rebecca on the toxic feelings associated with addictions that can adversely affect your life. We utilized the Internet to research the dangers associated with alcohol, marijuana and a junk food diet. An important point to remember with those suffering addictions is to educate them on the many ways that toxic addictions can hurt you.

Another way that ECT is a unique process is the aspect of focusing on "ever changing needs" that can cause one stress. For Rebecca, she needed time and support to comprehend the dangerous relationship needs she was involved in on a daily basis. I often ask my clients, "What's this relationship you are choosing doing for you? Are you fully informed about the dangers? This gives the client the power to make better decisions going forward.

Another key point to focus on relating to Rebecca's case was the occurrence of regression during the treatment process. Why? Addictions can be very powerful. It is rare that I see an individual recover in a short span from their addictions when they are experiencing a great deal of emotional and physical pain. Rebecca was no different. She had periods of growth but also some setbacks.

The goal of Emotional Core Therapy is to help clients identify the toxics feelings they experience in their daily life when they enter into an addictive relationship. This is not an overnight process. Oftentimes the treatment plan takes place over the course of weeks or several months. The reason that therapy can take extended periods of time is that addictions are learned behaviors that are acquired over the course of several months, even years. The human mind takes time to learn new behaviors both negative and positive. It can take several weeks or months to learn ECT, aside from relieving the suffering associated with addictions.

I shared with Rebecca the Greek fable of the young boy Icarus. Icarus was warned by his father to not travel too close to the sun with his wings made up of clay, wax and feathers. Icarus ignored the warning of his father and flew near the hot sun. His wings melted and he fell to the earth and perished. Individuals can seek temporary power, such like Icarus, from their addictions in order to escape the sufferings associated with negative feelings. ECT shows you how to gain genuine and long lasting power. This is done through having healthy relationships with yourself and others that bring the authentic feeling of joy.

To accomplish the treatment objective of finding real joy, Rebecca and I worked together to create a list of 10 relationships that would bring authentic joy into her life. Each week Rebecca and I worked together using ECT to establish the relationships on her treatment plan. Rebecca was close with her mother, Cheryl. Rebecca, Cheryl and I worked together to implement a positive and supportive treatment plan to provide motivation for Rebecca to use ECT to change her behaviors. The incentive in Rebecca's treatment plan was for Cheryl to pay for gas and insurance for Rebecca's vehicle.

Rebecca's father also played a role in the treatment process. The father would often use negative reinforcement and the possibility of negative consequences to influence a change in Rebecca's behavior. We worked with the father to help him see the negative effects that his communication methods had on Rebecca. The father's poor communication skills drove him away from Rebecca. They also hindered Rebecca's desire to make a change in her life by getting treatment. In therapy Rebecca was able to realize that she was internalizing her feelings of fear from her father, and turning to substances for temporary relief.

Over time Rebecca was able to gain power over her addictive behavior. She was becoming more aware that she was responsible for entering into her addictive relationships. (Step one of the ECT Flowchart). We looked at how entering relationships with ourselves, others people, places and things can cause stress in our life. Rebecca worked on changing her relationship with herself, her parents, her social network, and her addictions, to create a more emotionally balanced lifestyle.

The substances that Rebecca used to feed her addiction, such as alcohol, marijuana, and junk food adversely affected her body and mind. These substances have a physical makeup which cause harm to those like Rebecca, who digest or inhale it into their system. (Step two of ECT Flowchart)

Rebecca was able to realize that her body's ability to receive the same "high" from these substances was diminishing over time. Rebecca even spent four days in a treatment hospital to manage the physical effects associated with withdrawal from alcohol. Her five senses were being altered by her relationship with her addictions. (Step three of ECT Flowchart)

Using ECT, Rebecca and I were able to identify her authentic feeling of fear and grief relating to the addiction of the substances. Some of her emotional duress was caused by the expensive treatment and the physical pain that she endured. (Step four of the ECT Flowchart)

Rebecca became aware of these feelings and they became registered in her brain. (This is step five of the ECT Flowchart). Step five is a step that comes naturally to most people.

Being more aware of her feelings helped Rebecca gain power over her addictions and negative behavior. This allowed her to move forward with the treatment of ECT. Rebecca and I would review the flowchart weekly. Over time she gained a firm command of the ECT process. Having the flowchart at her hands was a safety net for Rebecca. She was able to identify her uncomfortable physical symptoms which included lack of sleep, irritability, stomach pain, digestive problems, and weight gain. She also identified crippling feelings of fear and grief. (Step six of the ECT Flowchart.)

Once we were able to eliminate the intake of negative substances into her body Rebecca began to feel better. The physical discomfort she had identified was slowly decreasing. Rebecca also began to release the toxic feelings of grief and fear from her addictions. (Step seven of the ECT Flowchart)

Rebecca was to maintain peace and balance in her daily life. We worked together to emphasize quiet time for reflection and meditation. She found ways to let her mind wander and freely float from thought to thought. When her life began to slow down for Rebecca she began to make better decisions for herself. (Step eight of the ECT Flowchart)

Meditation is a great way to care and respect your mind and body. I like to have clients such as Rebecca look back to a time in their life where they were most peaceful. Rebecca remembered when she was 12 years old when she would go to the lake with her family. She loved swimming and camping. We incorporated the same peace and balance that she experienced when she was 12, into her daily life as a young adult. Rebecca incorporated her love of nature by going on frequent walks with her dog, and jogging in the local parks as a way to relax. By taking this time for herself during her day she had greater success examining all of the relationships in her life.

Rebecca and her family were lifelong members of their local church. This facet of her life helped her deal with the challenges of her addiction in a number of ways. First, the teachings of her congregation stressed prohibitions against using alcohol and other drugs. Knowing that there was a moral issue involved, as well as physical and psychological, gave Rebecca added incentive to make the important changes that she knew she needed to make in her life. These teachings made it clear to Rebecca that it was God's will for her to overcome her addictions. Moreover, though the church taught that abusing alcohol and drugs was sinful, it also taught that God was forgiving. He understands human weaknesses and failings, and since Christ died for all of our transgressions, people could be forgiven of every possible sin. Moreover, and just as importantly, He will strengthen them to resist the temptation to continue in their sinful lifestyle.

When it came to meditation, Rebecca's upbringing almost instinctively led her to turn to the Bible, which is of course front and center in virtually all Christian denominations. She was delighted to recall that the first psalm in the Book of Psalms, in describing a righteous man, states: *his delight is in the law of the Lord, and on his law he meditates day and night.*

Another Bible verse that brought peace into Rebecca's life also came from the Psalms: *The Lord is close to the brokenhearted and saves those who are crushed in spirit.* In her deepest, darkest moments, she often felt that these words were spoken by God specifically for her benefit. This made perfect sense to Rebecca, because her church taught her that the Lord did indeed reach out and speak directly to His people, both as a community of faith and as individual believers, through His Word.

For Rebecca, such scriptures meant that delving into God's word, and reading it in a spiritual way was the best method of meditation, and would bring her closer to God. She spoke to her pastor, and he pointed her to numerous other biblical passages that spoke of the power of meditation, and showed her how prayerfully reflecting on the Bible and its message of redemption and healing could help lead to her recovery.

Initially Rebecca rated her level of emotional pain at a nine on a one to ten scale. Using ECT, Rebecca was able to reduce her emotional and physical suffering down to a level of two for most of her day. Each person is different in their level of self-awareness. Rebecca had a sense of accomplishment that she had grown through examining and changing her relationships.

Another case of a successful resolution to an addiction problem was found in the case of Duane. Duane lived with his mom, dad, and older sister and worked as an electrician during the day. When he came to me, he was clearly suffering from substance abuse and anger management issues. He was arrested for a DUI which resulted into legal and financial strain. He was required to hire an attorney and pay assigned court fines as well as lose his driving privileges. Duane was also arrested for Assault during a bar fight only three months after his DUI arrest. He was very fearful of going to jail so he began to seek out counseling as treatment for his emotional duress. Duane and I worked together several times a week, over a period of three months, to learn how to apply ECT as a way to deal with his emotional stress that was spiraling out of control. Duane's heavy drinking was a result of his feelings of rejections by his father over his career choice as an electrician. Duane's father was a successful business man and looked down upon a position in the skilled trades.

Duane's father spent his money lavishly on Duane's mother and sister. Over time Duane perceived himself as the black sheep of the family as he was often excluded from family functions. Duane did not dare show his anger towards his father. He found himself acting out in fist fights with strangers over trivial matters. When he went to court for the events related to his substance abuse, the judge expressed his desire for an immediate change in Duane's lifestyle or face the consequence of time in jail. In our treatment sessions, Duane and I were able to identify the anger and violent acts he displayed was related to his father. This unresolved anger towards his father was the underlying cause for Duane's emotional pain. We began to process feelings of grief during therapy by utilizing several of the ECT techniques discussed in this book to release the toxic feelings in Duane's life.

One method that we used in therapy which was not discussed in previous chapters is the technique of using psychodrama. Psychodrama is an action method of therapy which uses dramatization and role playing to gain insight into the individual's behavior. By acting out his feeling of rejection by his father out in a psychodrama scene, Duane was finally able to make sense of his emotional pain. He suffered from a combination of mental health and substance abuse issues. ECT helped treat both emotional problems.

Though Duane's family was never particularly religious, when he was in high school, as part of a History assignment Duane had learned about the development of ancient Christianity. The more he read about Christian beliefs and practices, Duane became intrigued by it. He realized that this ageless wisdom could help bring a strong measure of peace and balance into his often tumultuous life.

Now, as Duane started using ECT, he began relying on Christian principles even more as he learned healthy ways to release his emotions. For example, the Bible teaches that letting go of worry is easy when you place all of your faith in God. In Philippians 4:12-13, Duane read the following: "I know what it is to be in need, and I know what it is to have plenty. I have learned the secret of being content in any and every situation, whether well fed or hungry, whether living in plenty or in want. [1]I can do all this through him who gives me strength." Such comforting passages helped Duane to relax and let his mind enter a meditative state. He no longer felt so trapped by his circumstances, which, along with ECT helped him to start dealing with his anger issues in healthier ways.

As Duane continued to learn more about Jesus, especially by faithfully reading the Bible, he embraced the faith wholeheartedly. It teaches that the universe works harmoniously according to the laws set forth by its Creator. We reap what we sow. Therefore, when a person asserts their will in ways that are contrary to this harmony (i.e., against God's will), it causes all kinds of personal disruptions and problems. Duane could really identify with this, because he had been experiencing so much turmoil in his own life.

Emotional Core therapy was a good fit for Duane for many other reasons, too. For example, we were able to apply the psychological techniques of ECT to all of his relationship issues. We spent some time in therapy discussing his anger and other times discussing his substance abuse issues. Using the ECT flow chart, Duane was able to regain power over his life. Reviewing the flowchart each week was an efficient way to monitor his emotional state. Duane was able to identify the self-defeating habits that were the root cause of his legal and financial trouble. Duane's father was not willing to change his behaviors that were hurting him. It was going to be up to Duane to decide what kind of relationship he wanted with his angry father. By using ECT, Duane and I were able to identify the reality that minimized contact with his father was a healthy way to limit that cause of grief in his life.

Duane began to spend more time outside the home as a way to create distance from his father. Duane also kept the dialogue and conversation with his father at a minimum. This lowered Duane's level of anger. As we mentioned in chapter four, anger is a reaction to grief. The more that Duane was able to identify and process his grief, the quicker he was able to move towards healthier relationships. When Duane was outside the home he began to talk with the neighbors and began to connect with them on an improved level for support and friendship. Duane also began to take walks into town and visit more places. He enjoyed his tiny new discoveries and felt proud of himself for trying something new and different. I often tell my clients when God closes a door, He opens a window. It is my way of showing optimism and hope to people that are making tough relationship choices along with changes in their lives.

To help the reader examine the emotional growth of Duane in therapy I will again use the ECT Flowchart. By using the ECT Flowchart the reader can see the learning process that entails working in therapy. Nothing is easy in life that is worthwhile. As we read in God's Word, we all have our crosses to bear. Sometimes working on an individual step of ECT can take weeks or months, depending on the severity of the problem. As we mentioned previously, there are five or six main components of the ECT Flowchart that require work and insight into how to learn. Several of the steps happen to most of us very quickly. Another important point to remember is that some people have knowledge and ability in one or two steps and need help on certain other steps. People have to assess their own ability and knowledge in and open and honest fashion. Therapy can help in that process.

Getting back to Duane's case, we examined that Duane's toxic relationship with his dad was causing his anger. (Step one of the ECT Flowchart was understanding he had entered into a new relationship.)

The reason this was hard for Duane was that the father had emotional and financial needs that Duane was not able to meet. Duane's father would leave him out of family functions or belittle him in front of family and friends. (Step two of the ECT Flowchart was understanding that new relationships bring new needs from others.)

Duane would sense his father's ill will towards him through his senses. He would see and hear complaints periodically throughout the week. (Step three of the ECT Flowchart was understanding how we examine stress through our senses.)

This brought up feelings of fear and anger/grief with Duane. (Step Four of the ECT Flowchart was understanding how we authentically feel when stress hits us.)

A consistent message of fear and grief was sent to Duane's brain when he was near his angry father. (Step five of the ECT Flowchart tells us what each feeling signals to our brain.)

Duane felt uptight, stressed out, and agitated around his father. (Step Six of the ECT Flowchart tells us what bodily symptoms occur when we feel stress.)

Duane was unable to show his feelings towards his father as he felt ashamed and weak. He had his own ways of dealing with this at home. Sometimes he would squeeze his stress ball. Sometimes he would punch a punching bag. Sometimes he would go out and yell and scream in the backyard. These were all ways that Duane used to "externalize" his feelings. In our counseling sessions we used some common psychological techniques mentioned earlier in the book to release stress like journaling and assertiveness training. This step is crucial to understanding the ECT process. Why? We are constantly cathartically releasing stress throughout the day. Emotionally healthy people do this to cleanse their soul. (Step Seven of the ECT Flowchart is the releasing process. Learning to discharge feelings.)

Over time Duane learned to find quiet time for himself during the day to meditate and relax. This allowed him to regain a sense of himself. We revisited earlier times in his life when he relaxed such as bowling. When Duane bowled he was able to let his mind wander and daydream. His thoughts would be free floating and he became relaxed. It is important to note others may find bowling stressful. That is why you have to research each individual's past to see what suits them best. Duane would use bowling along with other meditative exercises to self soothe himself. (Step Eight of the ECT Flowchart is to balance your equilibrium.)

It is important to note we would do this ECT process for some of Duane's other relationship problems like alcohol and violence towards others. As you can see from reading the case of Duane and others in this book it takes time and energy to work through tough emotional states. This is all the more reason to be supportive of anyone who is going through a lifestyle change.

Throughout our counseling sessions I would have Duane rate his level of emotional pain. As we made inroads into

Duane's relationship stressors his level of pain dropped considerably. Having clients rate themselves is a great way to monitor their growth in therapy. It is rare I see someone go straight to recovery from a nine or ten to a one. Usually there is some back and forth movement. That is all the more reason to be kind to yourself while you are learning to understand emotions.

As we near the finish line in our book I want to remind the reader again of the character Dorothy in the movie, "The Wizard of Oz". Dorothy went through tremendous fear and grief when she left Kansas for the Land of Oz. Leaving the comforts of family and loved ones can open up a world of emotions for us as human beings. Some of these relationships are positive moments for emotional growth. Unfortunately, some relationships end up hurting our emotional well-being. The world is a unique discovery for all of us as adults. My hope is that each and every one of us lives life to its fullest. That we carry on all of our pursuits with passion and vitality.

Dorothy reminds all of us that family support is a priority in life. Dorothy clicked her heels and repeated the mantra, "There is no place like home. There is no place like home." She reinforces those values over and over in her mind to commit them to memory. Emotional Core Therapy follows a similar line of thinking. Learn to love yourself and honor your feelings. Be genuine and authentic with your feelings. Learn from your emotions rather than running away from them. ECT teaches us to treasure and respect our unique spirit as human beings. Each human being is a beautiful creation.

List Your Possible Relationships that can be Addictive

   a) GOING TO THE CASINO

   b) GOING ON SHOPPING SPREE

   1)

   2)

   3)

   4)

   5)

List Negative Consequences that can result from Addictions

A) FINANCIAL TROUBLES

B) LEGAL TROUBLES

1)

2)

3)

4)

5)

List Negative Physical Symptoms that can Occur with Addictions

A) DIGESTIVE PROBLEMS

B) SLEEPING PROBLEMS

1)

2)

3)

4)

5)

List Ways to Release Symptoms of Stress Associated with Addictions

A) VERBALIZATION OF FEELINGS

B) BEING ASSERTIVE

1)

2)

3)

4)

5)

List Ways that you can Soothe Yourself instead of Addictions

    A) TAKING THE DOG FOR A WALK

    B) GOING FOR A WALK IN THE PARK

    1)

    2)

    3)

    4)

    5)

EMOTIONAL CORE THERAPY TEST. Answers are at bottom of test. By doing this test you will allow your mind to have another way to commit the ECT process to your long term memory. If you are not sure of an answer, try and find the answer in the book. This will help you learn ECT. Also, the way to master the ECT approach is to retake the quiz by doing only the answers you incorrectly answered.

1) According to the ECT approach, the four authentic feelings that arise from relationship stress are?

A) Happiness, depression, fear, love

B) Joy, anxiety, sadness, anger

C) Joy, grief, fear, and relief

D) Joy, fear, anger, grief.

2) The predominant state of a person that has successfully learned ECT is?

A) Happiness, love, and lust

B) Assertiveness and calmness

C) Tranquility and balanced equilibrium

D) Loving and positive nature.

3) According to the ECT approach, the root cause of emotional stress is caused by?

A) Associating with angry and violent people

B) Being angry with your parents.

C) Holding onto anger in your body and Mind

D) Entering and leaving relationships that evoke one of the four true feelings.

4) According to the ECT approach, the four authentic feelings are?

A) Permanent states of being

B) Temporary states of being

C) Both permanent and temporary states of being

D) Neither permanent nor temporary states of being

5) According to the ECT approach, a healthy mind occurs when?

A) A person allows their mind time each day to meditate, daydream, and relax

B) A person holds onto feelings of grief and fear for several years

C) Learns to focus only on positive thoughts

D) Stays permanently away from negative people

6) The ECT Flowchart entails?

A) Five steps to learning to identify and process emotions

B) Six steps to identify and process emotions

C) Seven steps to identify and process emotions

D) Eight steps to identify and process emotions

7) According to ECT, relationships with ourselves or others usually involve which needs to be met?

A) Emotional, religious, physical, and financial

B) Emotional, financial, spiritual, and physical

C) Emotional, financial, spiritual, and sexual

D) Cognitive, financial, spiritual, and physical

8) The five senses needed to process emotions are

A) Seeing, touching, feeling, tasting, and listening

B) Believing, hearing, touching, tasting, and hearing

C) Hearing, touching, smelling, tasting, and seeing

D) Seeing, believing, touching, tasting, and hearing

9) When learning the ECT approach it is important to?

A). Focus on yourself and learn the ECT process by meditating three hours a day.

B). Focus on rewards and consequences to learn the ECT approach

C). Find a teacher to help you learn the ECT approach.

D). Be kind, supportive, and reward yourself to help learn the ECT approach

10) In order for ECT to be of real value, the process needs to be?

A) Available nearby so you can access the ECT Flowchart

B) Taught in most school aged classrooms

C) Taught as part of marital therapy

D) Learned and committed to one's long term memory through repetition

11) ECT emphasizes that stress can come to us hourly and daily. Therefore, we need to release these emotions hourly and daily as a learned habit like brushing your teeth. The "cleansing of the soul" is called?

A) Catharsis

B) Internalization

C) Suppression of emotions

D) Reflection

12) Feelings of sadness or unhappiness. Crying spells. Loss of interest or pleasure in normal activities. Fatigue, tiredness, and loss of energy. These are all symptoms of?

A) Anxiety

B) Anger

C) Depression

D) Addiction

13) In the case of Tina who suffered from depression, she was able to release her feelings through which techniques?

A). Cognitive Behavioral Therapy

B) Acceptance Commitment Therapy

C) Role playing and empty chair technique

D) Psychodrama

14) In the case of a Julie who suffered from depression after she lost her job when her company closed its doors, her symptoms included?

A) Feeling disturbed and disoriented.

B) Happy to get rid of her boss

C) Angry at the system

D) Fatigue, lack of sleep, and trouble concentrating

15) Gary, the construction worker in chapter two suffered from?

A) Anger towards his wife for not cooking dinner

B) Depression and isolation from his job in the family construction business

C) Anxiety from working in the finance field

D) Depression from his career as a golf pro

16) According to ECT, symptoms of anxiety include which of the following?

A) Having an increased heart rate, breathing rapidly, sweating, and trembling

B) Being angry throughout the day

C) Being assertive with your angry father

D) Losing hope and feeling suicidal

17) In the case of Drew who suffered from anxiety, he was given techniques to try and release his debilitating feelings of fear. These techniques included?

A) Listening to hip hop music on his headphones

B) Watching a football game

C) Writing, journaling, drawing, listening to music, exercising, jogging, meditation, yoga, or Pilates

D) Reading his horoscope daily

18). In the case of William who suffered from anxiety, ECT was able to?

A) Completely cure his anxiety

B) Not be any help at all

C) Reduce his stress in the short term to a level of 5 or 6 out of 10

D) Eliminate both his anger and his anxiety from his central nervous system for good

19) What exercise did William do to help reduce anxiety and oxygenate the blood in his body and improve his circulatory and digestive system?

A) Running

B) Golf

C) Weight lifting

D) Pilates

20) To help reduce Lillian's anxiety, ECT was used how?

A) ECT helped Lillian internalize her stress while at work

B) ECT was used to write down ten different ways she was overwhelmed and then worked to process those feelings

C) ECT was used to help her focus on a more lucrative career

D) ECT was used to help her understand her career interests

21) What ECT techniques did Lillian use to meditate and get her to a peaceful and calm state of being?

A) Lay on a couch and state out loud the first thing that came to her mind

B) Retrain her thoughts to only think positively

C) Stay away from any negative human beings

D) Taking short deep breathes and meditating in nature like when she was young

22) Some symptoms of anger are the following?

A) Feeling hopeless and not wanting to be with friends

B) Feeling tired all the time and not being able to sleep

C) Feeling hot, flushed and agitated. Tension in shoulders and neck

D) Not wanting to deal with conflict at home or work

23) According to ECT, anger is a reaction to which one of the four authentic feelings?

A) Joy

B) Grief

C) Fear

D) Relief

24) A way to gauge someone's success in learning ECT is to?

A) The more you can learn and acquire the steps of the ECT Flowchart the more confident you will feel about yourself

B) Learn to stay peaceful by smoking marijuana and obtain a lifestyle of meditation

C) Learn to control your anger at home and work at all times

D) Learn to only stay in relationships that bring you joy

25) Guilt happens when we hurt other human beings. The underlying authentic emotion of someone who is feeling guilty is?

A) Joy

B) Grief

C) Fear

D) Relief

26) According to ECT, the best ways to honor and respect your spouse or partner is to

A) Bring flowers and gifts at least once a week

B) Honor the four needs and four authentic feelings of your loved one

C) Be respectful to your partner's family and friends

D) Negotiate time to go on a date at least once a week

27) ECT is successful when used to help couples because of which of the following?

A) ECT can help gain autonomy for both partners by having them gain peace and vitality in their lives

B) ECT can cut in half the cost of marital therapy by resolving issues quickly once and for all

C) ECT can help couples dissolve relationships with former lovers who are still in the picture

D) ECT can eliminate all negativity from a couple's life while on vacation

28) The definition of an addiction is which of the following?

A) A need for something that you can't do without on a daily basis

B) A compulsive need to make money above all other priorities in your life

C) A compulsive physiological and psychological need for a habit forming substance

D) A desire to which you cannot control and for which you need professional help

29) Addictions, like in the case of Rebecca, can cause a variety of emotions to arise in an individual. Rebecca suffered from alcohol, marijuana, and junk food addictions. When her addictions controlled her life, which of the four authentic feelings were predominant in her mind?

A) Addictions ultimately bring relief and joy

B) Addictions ultimately bring grief and fear

C) Addictions ultimately bring anger and relief

D). Addictions ultimately bring anger and pain

30) Individuals seek temporary emotional power through the use of any addiction. ECT helps you find genuine and long lasting power by helping you find relationships that bring which authentic feeling?

A) Joy

B) Grief

C) Fear

D) Relief

Answers. 1) C. 2) C. 3) D. 4). B. 5). A. 6). D. 7). B. 8). C. 9). D. 10). D. 11). A. 12). C. 13). C. 14). D. 15) B. 16). A. 17). C. 18). C. 19). A. 20). B. 21). D. 22). C. 23). B. 24). A. 25). B. 26). B. 27). A. 28). C. 29). B. 30). A

IF YOU STILL NEED HELP LEARNING ECT DO THE FOLLOWING. MAKE A LIST BELOW OF TEN STRESSFUL EVENTS IN YOUR LIFE. JUST LIKE WE DID WITH DUANE AND REBECCA, PROCESS EACH OF THESE EVENTS USING THE EIGHT STEP ECT FLOWCHART.

1)

2)

3)

4)

5)

6)

7)

8)

9)

10)

ECT Flow Chart

> ### Relationships;
> self, other people, places, things

⬇

> ### Needs;
> emotional, financial, spiritual, physical

⬇

> ### Five Senses;
> seeing, touching, smelling, tasting, hearing

⬇

> ### Four Authentic Feelings;
> joy, grief, fear, relief

⬇

> ### Effects;
> brain/central nervous system

⬇

> ### Uncomfortable Symptoms;
> muscle tightness, fatigue, etc.

⬇

> ### Releasing Process;
> learn to discharge toxic feelings

⬇

> ### Balancing Your Equilibrium;
> practice various daily meditative techniques

Made in the USA
Middletown, DE
01 August 2016